ENGLAND RUGBY

THE OFFICIAL YEARBOOK
2014/15

This edition published in 2015

Carlton Books Limited
20 Mortimer Street
London W1T 3JW

A CIP catalogue record for this book is
available from the British Library.

10 9 8 7 6 5 4 3 2 1

ISBN 978-1-78097-659-4

Project director: Martin Corteel
Project Art Editor: Luke Griffin
Author: Iain Spragg
Picture research: Paul Langan
Book designer: Katie Baxendale
Editorial assistants: Chris Hawkes and
David Ballheimer
Production: Maria Petalidou

Printed in Slovenia

England Rugby

ENGLAND RUGBY

THE OFFICIAL YEARBOOK
2014/15

CARLTON BOOKS

Dave Attwood claims lineout ball for England in the QBE International against New Zealand.

Contents

FOREWORD BY:
Stuart Lancaster

England Rugby

Welcome to the 2014 edition of the official *Rugby England Yearbook*. I hope you enjoy it – there's certainly been plenty for England supporters to celebrate over the course of the last 12 months.

It was my third year as head coach, and although we suffered some setbacks along the way, I was incredibly proud of the team's commitment and, in particular, of our progress in the RBS 6 Nations as we claimed the Triple Crown for the first time since 2003.

The championship is a superb tournament that asks serious questions of each side, and to beat Ireland and Wales at Twickenham, as well as going to Murrayfield and beating Scotland, was hugely satisfying.

The Grand Slam eluded us after a late try in Paris turned what we hoped would be a victory into defeat, but the way the players bounced back to win the next four games spoke volumes about their collective character.

The QBE Internationals were both encouraging and frustrating. The narrow defeats to the All Blacks and the Springboks were disappointing, but I was delighted that the boys were able to sign off with a good win over the Wallabies.

The England women's side emulated the men with their own Triple Crown success in the 6 Nations, but that was only the beginning of an incredible 2014 for Gary Street and his side, and their triumph in the World Cup was a truly iconic moment for English rugby.

I was lucky enough to be sitting in the stands of the Stade Jean-Bouin in Paris to watch England beat Canada in the final, and their victory was magical after a 20-year wait to lift the trophy.

The women were not the only English world champions in 2014, and the Under-20 side did the country proud in June when they successfully defended their IRB Junior World Championship crown in Auckland, beating the Springboks in the final.

As the old saying goes, it's harder to defend a title than to win it for the first time, and it was a great effort from Nick Walshe's squad to head to New Zealand and justify their billing as the world's number one side.

As a coach, I am really excited about the opportunity to work with some of the Under-20 players when they graduate to the senior set-up over the next few years. Their success bodes well for the future, and is further evidence that our system continues to produce world-class talent.

The women's and Under-20s' triumphs, of course, only make me, the rest of the England coaches and the players even more desperate for success in the World Cup on home soil in 2015. We know there are big expectations of us as a group, not least from ourselves, and we are determined not to let people down.

Best wishes,
Stuart Lancaster

Right: **Stuart Lancaster hopes to lead England to World Cup glory in 2015.**

England and New Zealand line up before the start of the opening QBE International at Twickenham.

Introduction

England
Rugby

By any measure of success, 2014 was a year in which England sides excelled on the international stage. Three major trophies were proudly placed in the trophy cabinet at Twickenham in just six months and England's teams prospered at all levels of the game.

In 2013, it was the Under-20s who had flown the flag for English rugby with a famous success in the IRB Junior World Championship in France; 12 months later, the senior men and women emulated the young pretenders with their own triumphs and tangible silverware.

The catalyst came in March, when Stuart Lancaster's team beat Wales at Twickenham in the final round of matches in the RBS 6 Nations. Their 28–19 victory at HQ not only avenged the defeat they had suffered in Cardiff 12 months earlier, a result which had denied England the Grand Slam, but also sealed the Triple Crown for the first time in more than a decade.

Below: **England's Under-20 side were crowned IRB Junior World Champions in New Zealand.**

Above: **England's Women lifted the World Cup for a second time in 2014.**

English rugby's bright future was highlighted in June, when the Under-20 side journeyed to New Zealand to defend their coveted IRB crown. A dramatic 21–20 victory over South Africa in the final at Eden Park in Auckland ensured the young stars returned home with the trophy once again, and with three of the side that had triumphed in France in 2013 already elevated to Lancaster's senior squad, the England head coach now has another rich crop of new talent at his disposal.

In August, England's women travelled to France for the World Cup. Gary Street's side had already emulated the men in claiming the Triple Crown in the RBS 6 Nations, but after the anguish of defeat in the three previous World Cup finals, the team's overriding ambition was to become world champions. England fought their way to the final, and it was a heady mixture of euphoria and sheer relief that greeted the final whistle in Paris after the side's 21–9 victory over Canada.

It was also a watershed year for the women's game with the advent of professionalism; 20 of England's leading lights have become full-time players, centrally contracted to the Rugby Football Union, putting them on a level footing with their male counterparts for the first time.

As the year drew to a close, thoughts inevitably turned to the eighth instalment of the World Cup in England in 2015. It will be the second time the country has hosted the tournament, and with an estimated three million supporters attending the games, and a worldwide television audience in the billions, it promises to be the biggest and most global World Cup yet.

Mike Brown breaches
the New Zealand
defence during
England's narrow first
Test defeat at Auckland
in June 2014.

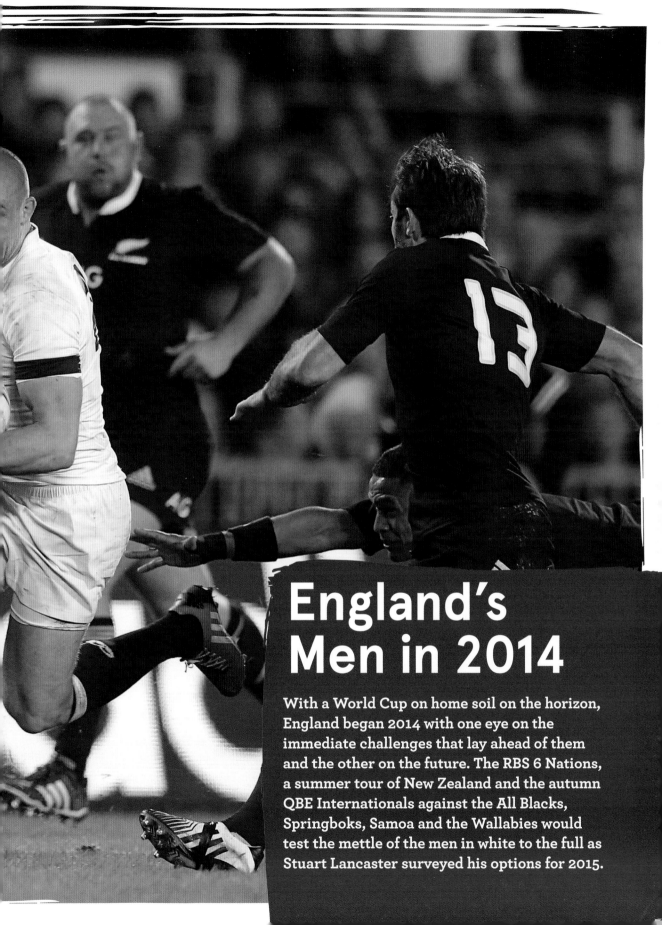

England's Men in 2014

With a World Cup on home soil on the horizon, England began 2014 with one eye on the immediate challenges that lay ahead of them and the other on the future. The RBS 6 Nations, a summer tour of New Zealand and the autumn QBE Internationals against the All Blacks, Springboks, Samoa and the Wallabies would test the mettle of the men in white to the full as Stuart Lancaster surveyed his options for 2015.

England captain Chris Robshaw (right) leads the players round the pitch after the 13–10 victory against Ireland in the RBS 6 Nations Championship at Twickenham on 22 February.

RBS 6 Nations 2014

England may have been denied a famous Grand Slam in 2013 after a chastening defeat to Wales at the Millennium Stadium in the climax of the championship, but a youthful Red Rose prepared for the 120th instalment of European rugby's showpiece competition the following year undaunted and unbowed.

It was Stuart Lancaster's third 6 Nations campaign as head coach since succeeding Martin Johnson and, despite a last-gasp loss in the tournament opener against France, it was to prove one of his most successful yet.

RBS 6 NATIONS TABLE 2014

Pos	Team	P	W	D	L	PF	PA	Tries	PTS
1	Ireland	5	4	0	1	132	49	16	8
2	England	5	4	0	1	138	56	14	8
3	Wales	5	3	0	2	122	79	11	5
4	France	5	3	0	2	101	100	9	6
5	Scotland	5	1	0	4	47	138	4	2
6	Italy	5	0	0	5	63	172	7	0

France vs England

AGONY IN PARIS

England
Rugby

FRA 26

ENG 24

Date: **1 February 2014**
Stadium: **Stade de France, Saint-Denis**
Attendance: **78,763**
Referee: **Nigel Owens (Wales)**

Searching for a first championship title since 2011 and a first Triple Crown triumph in 11 years, England began their bid for silverware in 2014 with a tough opening assignment against Philippe Saint-André's France. The Red Rose had emerged victors in their two previous RBS 6 Nation clashes with *Les Bleus*, including a 24–22 win in Paris in 2012, but they were dramatically denied a third successive victory over the French after a devastating late coup de grâce in the Stade de France.

It was ahead of his first game as England head coach, the 2012 RBS 6 Nations clash with Scotland in Edinburgh, that Stuart Lancaster set the tone for his new regime. Lancaster wanted England to become both fearless and feared and he signalled his intent to radically overhaul the side by naming seven new caps for the match at Murrayfield.

It was a bold decision rewarded with a 13–6 victory in the Scottish capital, and since then the head coach has continued to reinvigorate and remould the team as he strives to return England to the pinnacle of the world game.

It came as no surprise then that Lancaster was willing to hand Test debuts to 20-year-old Exeter Chiefs wing Jack Nowell and Northampton centre Luther Burrell, 26, for the opening RBS 6 Nations game of the season against France. The cauldron of the Stade de France, he insisted, would hold no fears for his debutants and the time had come to blood a new generation of England players.

Left: (L–R) Captains Pascal Pape of France and Chris Robshaw of England lead the teams out during the RBS 6 Nations at the Stade de France.

Above left: **Centre Luther Burrell goes over to score England's second try during the RBS 6 Nations clash with France at the Stade de France.**

Above right: **England No.8 Billy Vunipola breaks away from Yannick Nyanga of France to set off on one of his barnstorming runs.**

There was also a second cap for Gloucester's Jonny May on the left wing in "Le Crunch", eight months after making his international bow against Argentina in Buenos Aries, and a recall for Danny Care at scrum-half, his first start for his country in almost a year.

"Jack [Nowell] and Luther [Burrell] deserve their chance, as does Jonny May, who will be starting his first 6 Nations game," Lancaster said in the build-up to the match. "I've always believed if a player's ready and deserving an opportunity, then we need to give it to them. You've got to make a debut at some point.

"Danny [Care] suffered the disappointment of not being involved in the first game in the autumn. We gave him some areas to work on – his game management, his kicking game – and he's gone away and done that."

The stage was set for the 98th cross-Channel clash between the two countries. France, for their part, were desperate to banish the embarrassing memories of collecting the Wooden Spoon in 2013 and the atmosphere in Paris before kick-off was an intriguing mixture of anticipation and nervousness in the massed ranks of the home support.

Luck though is a notoriously fickle commodity in sport, and it was France who enjoyed all of it in the opening 17 minutes. England's defence was breached after just 32 seconds when Jules Plisson's chip was deflected and fell fortuitously for Yoann Huget to storm over for the first try of the match. The home side went further ahead when another French kick – this time from Brice Dulin – bounced outrageously to evade both Nowell and Alex Goode and present Huget with another gift-wrapped scoring opportunity.

Trailing 16–3 after a Jean-Marc Doussain penalty, England were on the ropes, but the fightback that ensued spoke volumes about the character and inner steel of Lancaster's side.

The first English riposte came five minutes before the break ,when the reinstated Care took a quick tap penalty deep in enemy territory and scampered towards the line. As the defence converged on him, the scrum-half found full-back Mike Brown, who crashed through a tangle of French tacklers and muscled his way over for the opening try.

The visitors headed to the dressing room 16–8 in arrears, but emerged for the second half with ferocity and fire, and seven minutes after the restart they silenced the Stade de France by taking the lead. Fly-half Owen Farrell landed an early penalty and when No.8 Billy Vunipola punched a gaping hole in the heart of the midfield with a rampaging charge that saw him commit three French tacklers, Burrell was the man on hand to turn the incursion into points, taking the perfectly timed pass from the Saracens forward to race free under the posts on debut. Farrell landed the routine conversion and the Red Rose were now 18–16 ahead.

England had never before come from more than 12 points behind to win a Test

Left: **Gael Fickou of France goes over to score a try during the RBS 6 Nations match.**

Right: **A dejected Dylan Hartley (L) and captain Chris Robshaw of England leave the field after their RBS 6 Nations defeat to France.**

match, but they appeared to be poised to rewrite history when the irrepressible Care slotted a 56th-minute drop goal to extend the advantage. France replied with a Maxime Machenaud penalty, only for Goode to kick another three points for England. With just eight minutes remaining on the clock, Lancaster's team were 24–19 leaders.

The tension in the Stade de France was palpable and *Les Tricolores* came at England in the dying minutes with the desperation that only a side facing defeat and needing a try to rescue themselves can know. England initially repelled the inevitable wave of attacks, but the French finally broke through the wall of white shirts for the decisive score in the 76th minute.

The home side won possession on halfway and moved the ball wide left. A pass in midfield eventually found its way to replacement hooker Dimitri Szarzewski, who charged down the touchline as the England defence desperately tried to get across. Brown moved forward to make the tackle on the

French front rower, but Szarzewski was able to offload to fellow substitute Gael Fickou before contact and with France suddenly presented with a two-on-one overlap, the young Toulouse wing deftly dummied Goode. There was no cover left and Fickou, who had only been on the pitch for two minutes after coming off the bench to replace Mathieu Bastareaud, was able to canter over the whitewash unchallenged and dot the ball down near the posts.

The Stade de France erupted with relief. The crucial conversion was a formality for Machenaud and heartbreaking for England and France had dramatically snatched victory from the jaws of defeat in Paris, claiming a 26–24 win.

The look of abject dejection on the faces of the England players after the final whistle told its own story, but Lancaster was eager to emphasize the strength of character displayed by his team in defeat.

The head coach said in his post-match interview: "Once we get over the initial disappointment we'll take a huge amount of positives from the game Games are never won or lost in one moment. Everything matters at this level. It was a great Test match played by two great teams.

"At the start we put ourselves into a bit of a hole, but I thought the boys showed incredible character, resilience and a lot of skill to put ourselves in a position to win it. But a bit of French flair at the end and they got the win. We're very disappointed to lose like that.

"It was a good place to come. I thought our young players learned a lot and I'm very proud of them. Overall the positives of the performance will outweigh the result, but we recognize we need to win big games. Five of our pack made their first start in France. They were the youngest pack in the championship and they did extremely well."

> "We've learned a lot from this game. We dominated the middle third and to claw our way back from 16–3 was great."
>
> **Stuart Lancaster**

France 26		England 24	
15	Brice DULLIN	15	Mike BROWN
14	Yoann HUGET	14 →	Jack NOWELL
13 →	Mathieu BASTAREAUD	13	Luther BURRELL
12	Wesley FOFANA	12	Billy TWELVETREES
11	Maxime MEDARD	11 →	Jonny MAY
10	Jules PLISSON	10	Owen FARRELL
9 →	Jean-Marc DOUSSAIN	9 →	Danny CARE
1 →	Thomas DOMINGO	1 →	Joe MARLER
2 →	Benjamin KAYSER	2 →	Dylan HARTLEY
3 →	Nicolas MAS	3	Dan COLE
4 →	Alexandre FLANQUART	4	Joe LAUNCHBURY
5	Pascal PAPE (c)	5 →	Courtney LAWES
6 →	Yannick Nyanga KABASELE	6	Tom WOOD
7	Bernard LE ROUX	7	Chris ROBSHAW (c)
8 →	Louis PICAMOLES	8 →	Billy VUNIPOLA

REPLACEMENTS		REPLACEMENTS	
2 ←	16 Dimitri SZARZEWSKI	2 ←	16 Tom YOUNGS
1 ←	17 Yannick FORESTIER	1 ←	17 Mako VUNIPOLA
3 ←	18 Rabah SLIMANI		18 Henry THOMAS
4 ←	19 Yoann MAESTRI	5 ←	19 Dave ATTWOOD
6 ←	20 Antoine BURBAN	8 ←	20 Ben MORGAN
8 ←	21 Damien CHOULY	9 ←	21 Lee DICKSON
9 ←	22 Maxime MACHENAUD	11 ←	22 Brad BARRITT
13 ←	23 Gael FICKOU	14 ←	23 Alex GOODE

SCORES	SCORES
Tries: **Huget** (1, 17), **Fickou** (76)	Tries: **Brown** (36), **Burrell** (47)
Con: **Machenaud** (78)	Con: **Farrell** (48)
Pens: **Doussain** (10, 22), **Machenaud** (69)	Pens: **Farrell** (5, 42), **Goode** (72)
	Drop: **Care** (56)

France		England
37	Kicks from hand	34
130	Passes	169
116	Runs	150
460	Metres run with ball	645
41%	Possession	59%
37%	Territory	63%
10	Clean breaks	8
26	Defenders beaten	28
17	Offloads	15
70 from 74	Rucks won	109 from 115
3 from 5	Mauls won	5 from 5
23	Turnovers conceded	21
151/27	Tackles (made/missed)	116/26
85.0%	Tackling success rate	82.0%
7 won, 0 lost, (100.0%)	Scrums on own feed	3 won, 2 lost, (60.00%)
10 won, 1 lost, (90.9%)	Lineouts on own throw	13 won, 2 lost, (86.7%)
4 (0)	Penalties conceded (freekicks)	8 (1)
0/0	Yellow/red cards	0/0

Scotland vs England

CALCUTTA CUP GLORY

England Rugby

SCO 0
ENG 20

Date: 8 February 2014
Stadium: Murrayfield,
Edinburgh
Attendance: 67,100
Referee: Jerome Garces
(France)

The oldest international fixture on the rugby calendar, the 132nd cross-border battle between England and Scotland saw both sides licking their wounds before kick-off following defeats in their championship openers. The Red Rose may have been unbeaten in their last six meetings against the oldest of enemies, but Stuart Lancaster was acutely aware that defeat at Murrayfield would abruptly end England's title aspirations.

A week may indeed be a long time in politics, but the seven days granted to England after their heartbreak in Paris prior to the clash with Scotland in Edinburgh was precious little time in which to recover mentally and physically. Test rugby is rarely forgiving, and Lancaster and his squad had to dust themselves off quickly.

There was good news on the injury front, however. The cheekbone Courtney Lawes had damaged against the French was deemed to be no worse than bruised, while Jonny May's fractured nose would not keep him out of the fray. The second row and winger were both declared fit for duty.

The temptation to make changes in the wake of defeat is always strong, but Lancaster resisted, naming an unchanged XV for the match. The coach had faith in his players to turn the tide and they were to respond magnificently.

"It's good to be able to select the same players and they are all determined to put last week's result behind them and build on the performance," Lancaster said. "Scotland will be hugely motivated by their defeat in Dublin and, as we found two years ago, Murrayfield is a tough place to play."

England's task was not made any easier by the state of the parasite-plagued Murrayfield pitch. An unwelcome infestation of nematodes had gripped the grass in

Below left: The pitch at Murrayfield was in poor condition ahead of England's RBS 6 Nations clash with Scotland.

Below: Luther Burrell stretches out to score after 14 minutes of the Calcutta Cup match in Edinburgh.

Above: **Full-back Mike Brown in full flow en route to scoring England's second try against Scotland at Murrayfield.**

Edinburgh and the pre-match debate was dominated by talk of how badly the pitch would cut up. England were warned to expect muddy trench warfare rather than a feast of fluid rugby.

Murrayfield did indeed resemble something of a quagmire at the end of the 80 minutes, but the Red Rose were ultimately unperturbed by the conditions under foot as they put Scotland to the sword.

England took a lead they were never to relinquish as early as the fifth minute. The pack did the abrasive work up front and when the ball was presented on a plate to Danny Care, the scrum-half opted for the drop goal with his right boot and saw his effort sail handsomely between the uprights.

The forwards were already comprehensively on top of their opposite numbers in blue and the first try came in the 14th minute after another destructive drive deep in the Scotland 22. As ever, Care was waiting at the back for the ball, and when it was duly delivered he set off on a lateral run. The defence initially seemed to have the danger covered, until Luther Burrell

appeared on a powerful charge back on the angle, taking Care's beautifully weighted pass and bursting through two despairing tackles for his second try in only his second Test appearance. Owen Farrell made no mistake with the conversion, as well as adding a 28th-minute penalty, and England powered their way into a 13–0 lead.

It could, perhaps should, have been an even greater advantage. A delightful dummy and midfield break from Farrell seconds before the break saw England again surge behind the Scottish defence. Burrell was on Farrell's shoulder to take the inside pass, but as the try line beckoned, he was hauled down inches short by an incredible last-gasp tackle by Scotland wing Tommy Seymour. England desperately tried to recycle the ball, but to no avail, and with the clock showing the allotted first 40 minutes were over, referee Jérôme Garces blew for half-time.

It was a similar story of so near and yet so far ten minutes after the restart. A trademark charge from Billy Vunipola made the first inroads and Mike Brown then sent Scotland scampering further back with a second thrust.

The ball was sent wide through the hands of Care, Farrell and Billy Twelvetrees to make space for May on the touchline, but he was dragged down just a metre shy of the try line.

It was merely to be a temporary reprieve for the Scots, however. Centre Alex Dunbar was sent to the sin bin for killing the ball in the melee that followed May's near miss and, seven minutes later, England made the most of their numerical superiority, scoring the try that ended the match as a contest.

The attack began with a muscular drive by prop Joe Marler in midfield. The pack secured possession, Care probed around the fringes of the Scottish defence and, although May's pass in the tackle went to ground, England were alert enough to pounce on the loose ball in the shape of Jack Nowell. Tight on the touchline, and faced by three Scottish players, the wing seemed to have nowhere to go, but a sudden burst of pace and some deft footwork took him past the first line of tacklers and left him sprinting towards the line. Scotland full-back Stuart Hogg blocked his path, but Brown was on his outside shoulder to take the crucial pass from Nowell, galloping over for his second try of the RBS 6 Nations. Farrell was successful with the

easy conversion and the Red Rose were 20 unanswered points in front.

A quarter of the match still remained. England's comprehensive dominance of both possession and territory continued but, despite playing with ambition and width, they were unable to pierce Scotland for a third try and Lancaster and his side had to content themselves with a successful defence of the Calcutta Cup courtesy of a 20-0 triumph.

It was the first time Scotland had failed to trouble the scoresheet in an international since 1978 (a 15-0 victory to England at Murrayfield) and it was the first time the Red Rose had kept a clean sheet since their 70-0 demolition of Canada at Twickenham a decade earlier.

"We were pleased with a lot of aspects, but are frustrated that we didn't convert more of our opportunities."

Stuart Lancaster

Above: **The victorious England players celebrate with the Calcutta Cup after their 20–0 triumph over Scotland.**

Opposite: **Owen Farrell contributed seven points with the boot as Engalnd registered their first win in the 2014 RBS 6 Nations championship.**

Scotland 0	England 20
15 Stuart HOGG	15 Mike BROWN
14 → Tommy SEYMOUR	14 Jack NOWELL
13 Alex DUNBAR	13 → Luther BURRELL
12 → Matt SCOTT	12 Billy TWELVETREES
11 Sean LAMONT	11 → Jonny MAY
10 Duncan WEIR	10 Owen FARRELL
9 → Greg LAIDLAW (c)	9 → Danny CARE
1 → Ryan GRANT	1 → Joe MARLER
2 → Ross FORD	2 → Dylan HARTLEY
3 → Moray LOW	3 → Dan COLE
4 Tim SWINSON	4 → Joe LAUNCHBURY
5 → Jim HAMILTON	5 Courtney LAWES
6 Ryan WILSON	6 Tom WOOD
7 Chris FUSARO	7 Chris ROBSHAW (c)
8 → David DENTON	8 → Billy VUNIPOLA

REPLACEMENTS	REPLACEMENTS
2 ← 16 Scott LAWSON	2 ← 16 Tom YOUNGS
1 ← 17 Alasdair DICKINSON	1 ← 17 Mako VUNIPOLA
3 ← 18 Geoff CROSS	3 ← 18 Henry THOMAS
5 ← 19 Jonny GRAY	4 ← 19 Dave ATTWOOD
8 ← 20 John BEATTIE	8 ← 20 Ben MORGAN
9 ← 21 Chris CUSITER	9 ← 21 Lee DICKSON
12 ← 22 Duncan TAYLOR	13 ← 22 Brad BARRITT
14 ← 23 Max EVANS	11 ← 23 Alex GOODE

SCORES	SCORES
	Tries: **Burrell** (14), **Brown** (58)
	Cons: **Farrell** (15, 59)
	Pen: **Farrell** (28)
	Drop: **Care** (5)

Scotland		England
26	Kicks from hand	25
78	Passes	151
86	Runs	118
201	Metres run with ball	434
42%	Possession	58%
34%	Territory	66%
3	Clean breaks	10
11	Defenders beaten	27
6	Offloads	11
73 from 75	Rucks won	81 from 85
1 from 2	Mauls won	13 from 13
12	Turnovers conceded	14
127/27	Tackles (made/missed)	100/11
82.0%	Tackling success rate	90.0%
5 won, 0 lost (100.0%)	Scrums on own feed	6 won, 0 lost (100.00%)
7 won, 5 lost (58.3%)	Lineouts on own throw	22 won, 2 lost (91.7%)
16 (1)	Penalties conceded (freekicks)	7 (0)
1/0	Yellow/red cards	0/0

Impressive statistics from an English perspective perhaps, but the mood in the camp after full time in Edinburgh was reflective rather than wildly celebratory as the coaches and players alike dissected the performance and rued some of the scoring opportunities that had been spurned.

"It was a tough shift by all the guys in tough conditions," said captain Chris Robshaw. "We weren't too happy with our attack. I felt we left some points out there and these are things we need to keep learning.

"We got away with it today, [but] we might not get away with it next time. It's been a tough start. We've had two weeks on the road and we're looking forward to getting back to Twickenham."

The coach echoed his skipper's words. There were, Lancaster insisted, reasons to smile, but with unbeaten Ireland heading to London in a fortnight's time to contest the Millennium Trophy, he was wary of repeating such profligacy against the men in green.

"There were chances there that we didn't take," said Lancaster. "It does set us up for an important game against Ireland. Ireland have played two, won two and have played really well. But we're definitely out to win the tournament, even after the loss to France."

England vs Ireland

IRELAND DESPATCHED AT HQ

England Rugby

ENG 13

IRL 10

Date: **22 February 2014**
Stadium: **Twickenham,
London**
Attendance: **81,835**
Referee: Craig Joubert
(South Africa)

The pre-match predictions promised a titanic arm wrestle between England and Ireland in round three of the championship and, to the delight of those in white among the 81,835 capacity Twickenham crowd, that is just what the two sides produced. With Brian O'Driscoll making a record-equalling 139th Test appearance, Joe Schmidt's side had the clear edge in terms of big-match experience, but it was young legs that prevailed over old heads in south-west London, as England emerged from a bruising encounter with a significant, albeit slender, victory.

It was during Ireland's biannual descent on London back in 1988 that HQ first reverberated to a rendition of "Swing Low, Sweet Chariot". English rugby's anthem was born and the Twickenham faithful have greeted visiting teams with a collective chorus of the song ever since.

The choir had certainly been in good voice in 2012 when England romped to a 30-9 victory at HQ, but there were times in 2014 when the singing was conspicuous by its absence as Ireland threatened to record a fourth win in their last five visits to Twickenham. England ultimately ensured the home support did have cause to break into song with a 13-10 success, but as a tense second half unfolded, it was almost too close to call.

Stuart Lancaster made just one, enforced change to the starting XV that had

Left: **Ireland full-back Rob Kearney breaks through the England defence at Twickenham to score a try.**

demolished Scotland, drafting in Bath prop David Wilson in place of the injured Dan Cole. The match would be the tight head's 32nd cap for his country, but only his eighth international start. The headline-grabbing selection news, however, was the inclusion of uncapped 20-year-old Bath fly-half George Ford on the bench. It was another clear illustration of Lancaster's philosophy of bringing through young talent sooner rather than later.

"I think George's confidence has grown through the season with Bath and he played extremely well last week [against Exeter], so we think he's ready," the head coach said. "We'll wait and see how the game unfolds, but if he does get his opportunity, we know he's ready."

The 128th instalment of Anglo-Irish rugby rivalry began with a ferocity that did not abate, and in the sixth minute it was England who asked the first question when a charge from Billy Vunipola and a probe by Danny Care eventually worked space for Jonny May out wide. A sidestep from the wing took him over the line, but English joy quickly turned to disappointment when replays confirmed Conor Murray had knocked the ball from May's grasp before he was able to touch down.

Ireland replied with a near miss of their own, going through the phases in the England 22 before Johnny Sexton deployed the cross-field kick for Andrew Trimble. The Ireland wing took the high ball and evaded the initial tackle but, as the line beckoned, Tom Wood pulled him down and the danger passed.

The first and only points of the first half went to England. Courtney Lawes was upended in mid-air in a lineout and, although the penalty was on the edge of his range, Owen Farrell stepped forward to accept the three points and send England into the dressing room in front.

The second half began with a bang, and it was Ireland who supplied the pyrotechnics. The visitors, camped in England territory, moved the ball to a static Jamie Heaslip, who in turn found Rob Kearney arriving like a runaway train. The inside pass to the full-back was perfect and Kearney sliced through the defensive line and raced over underneath the posts. Sexton converted and Ireland had stolen the lead.

The momentum was with the visitors and they stretched further ahead in the 49th minute with a Sexton penalty. Farrell responded with his second penalty four minutes later, but Ireland still enjoyed a 10–6 advantage and the anxious home support were temporarily in no mood for "Swing Low, Sweet Chariot".

Below left: Danny Care of England celebrates after scoring against Ireland in the 56th minute of the RBS 6 Nations game at HQ.

Below right: Owen Farrell was on target with two penalties and a conversion in England's 13–10 win over the Irish.

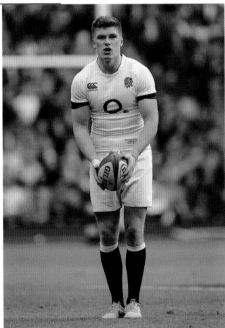

Left: **The match was Brian O'Driscoll's sixth and final visit to Twickenham as an Ireland player.**

England's pivotal response was both stylish and clinical. A ruck on their own 10-metre line gave Care possession at the base and he moved the ball to Billy Twelvetrees in midfield. The centre found skipper Chris Robshaw in support and, after making a half break, he slipped an inside pass to Mike Brown and, suddenly, England were behind Irish lines. Brown's searing pace took him all the way to the Ireland 10-metre line and as Kearney readied himself for the tackle, he looked to his right and saw Care on his shoulder. The pass was made and, although both Sexton and O'Driscoll were converging on him, the scrum-half had enough pace to score beneath the posts. Farrell stroked over the simple conversion and England were 13–10 to the good. Twickenham was alive with song once again.

A full 24 minutes remained, but it was testament to the discipline and commitment of both defences that no further points were scored. England went close through Jack Nowell, while the pack had to weather a nerve-shredding series of Ireland scrums and mauls late on, but Lancaster's team held firm to clinch victory.

The result threw the championship title race wide open, leaving England, Wales, Ireland and France with four points apiece after two wins from their opening three games. Ireland's unbeaten record was gone and, with a fourth consecutive victory over the Irish, the Red Rose had thrust themselves firmly back into contention.

It came as little surprise to the Twickenham faithful when Brown was named Man of the Match, but despite the accolade, the full-back's thoughts were already turning to the visit of Wales to HQ in two weeks' time.

"The lads were outstanding from 1 to 15 today, as well as the guys on the bench," he said. "We were pretty happy at half time, but we needed to finish off the phases. They were unbeaten and we wanted to set a marker.

"We'll go back into camp and work hard like we have before. Wales showed what they are about on Friday [against France]. They are going to be physical, they have got Lions players throughout their squad, so we're really going to have to turn up again. Hopefully the crowd will act as another 16th man for us like it did today."

Ireland head coach Joe Schmidt was left to rue what might have been after his side's narrow loss, but was magnanimous in defeat, paying tribute to Brown's impact on the outcome of the match.

"Mike Brown's goalkeeper save when there was no one behind him in the first half after our kick on, that was probably the defensive highlight, even without anyone having to make a tackle," Schmidt said. "And then his running

Opposite: **Mike Brown and Owen Farrell celebrate after England's hard-fought RBS 6 Nations victory over the Irish.**

in broken field was maybe the difference between the two teams. Mike Brown hit that line really well and they got away. They are the small instances in the game when things break open and, unfortunately for us, they broke open for England. It was very much a complete package from him today."

"That was a real Test match. Ireland are a quality team. It's fantastic to have won, and to get the reward at the end, given the commitment we have put in is really pleasing."

Stuart Lancaster

England 13	Ireland 10
15 Mike **BROWN**	15 Rob **KEARNEY**
14 Jack **NOWELL**	14 → Andrew **TRIMBLE**
13 Luther **BURRELL**	13 Brian **O'DRISCOLL**
12 Billy **TWELVETREES**	12 Gordon **D'ARCY**
11 Jonny **MAY**	11 Dave **KEARNEY**
10 Owen **FARRELL**	10 Johnny **SEXTON**
9 Danny **CARE**	9 → Conor **MURRAY**
1 → Joe **MARLER**	1 → Cian **HEALY**
2 → Dylan **HARTLEY**	2 → Rory **BEST**
3 → David **WILSON**	3 → Mike **ROSS**
4 Joe **LAUNCHBURY**	4 Devin **TONER**
5 Courtney **LAWES**	5 Paul **O'CONNELL** (c)
6 → Tom **WOOD**	6 → Peter **O'MAHONY**
7 Chris **ROBSHAW** (c)	7 → Chris **HENRY**
8 → Billy **VUNIPOLA**	8 Jamie **HEASLIP**

REPLACEMENTS	REPLACEMENTS
2 ← 16 Tom **YOUNGS**	2 ← 16 Sean **CRONIN**
1 ← 17 Mako **VUNIPOLA**	1 ← 17 Jack **McGRATH**
3 ← 18 Henry **THOMAS**	3 ← 18 Marty **MOORE**
6 ← 19 Dave **ATWOOD**	6 ← 19 Iain **HENDERSON**
8 ← 20 Ben **MORGAN**	7 ← 20 Jordi **MURPHY**
21 Lee **DICKSON**	9 ← 21 Isaac **BOSS**
22 George **FORD**	13 ← 22 Paddy **JACKSON**
23 Alex **GOODE**	14 ← 23 Fergus **McFADDEN**

SCORES

Try: **Care** (56)

Con: **Farrell** (56)

Pens: **Farrell** (24, 53)

SCORES

Try: **RDJ Kearney** (41)

Con: **Sexton** (42)

Pen: **Sexton** (49)

England		Ireland
20	Kicks from hand	24
124	Passes	192
107	Runs	122
424	Metres run with ball	364
41%	Possession	59%
47%	Territory	53%
5	Clean breaks	3
23	Defenders beaten	24
9	Offloads	4
72 from 79	Rucks won	101 from 108
6 from 9	Mauls won	7 from 10
13	Turnovers conceded	17
163/24	Tackles (made/missed)	117/23
87.0%	Tackling success rate	84.0%
5 won, 4 lost (55.65%)	Scrums on own feed	9 won, 0 lost (100.00%)
8 won, 0 lost (100.0%)	Lineouts on own throw	16 won, 0 lost (100.0%)
10 (1)	Penalties conceded (freekicks)	9 (0)
0/0	Yellow/red cards	0/0

England vs Wales

TRIPLE CROWN TRIUMPH

England
Rugby

ENG 29
WAL 18

Date: **9 March 2014**
Stadium: **Twickenham,
London**
Attendance: **82,000**
Referee: **Romain Poite
(France)**

Revenge is a word coaches and players studiously avoid before a Test match. And the England camp stuck obediently to the script as they prepared to face Wales at Twickenham, but just a year after the Grand Slam was cruelly wrestled from their grasp after a brutal demolition in Cardiff, putting that behind them with a win over the same opponents was top of the agenda.

The last time England had claimed the Triple Crown, Clive Woodward had yet to be dubbed "Sir", Martin Johnson was the skipper with the seemingly perpetual scowl, and the Red Rose were still eight months shy of lifting the World Cup in Sydney. Back in 2003, few would have predicted that 11 long and frustrating years would pass before an England side completed another Home Nations clean sweep.

The penultimate round of the 2014 championship finally presented Stuart Lancaster and his team with the opportunity to end the drought. Scotland and Ireland had already been despatched and now only Wales could spoil the planned party at HQ.

In the build-up , the England squad and head coach were bombarded by questions about their 30–3 mauling at the Millennium Stadium 12 months earlier, but the collective side-step of any talk of revenge was deft.

"This is being hyped up as an emotional revenge game, but as a team we haven't talked about that," insisted hooker Dylan Hartley.

Left: **Luther Burrell's try against Wales at Twickenham was his third for England in only his fourth Test appearance.**

"That day in Cardiff was the complete, all-round poor performance [from England] and we haven't seen anything like it since.

"The lesson has been learned and we don't need to prove it against Wales, because since then we have performed really well. I'm very aware that there's a massive rivalry between England and Wales and it's very historical. As a barometer, this is a good game for us."

Lancaster was compelled to make just one change to the team that had edged out Ireland. An ankle injury ruled out Billy Vunipola and Gloucester No.8 Ben Morgan was promoted from the bench as England looked to end a three-match losing sequence against their rivals from the Principality.

Wales arrived in London with 12 Lions in their ranks, but any sense of trepidation the England fans may have been experiencing was dispelled when Danny Care breached the red defence with just four minutes gone. Owen Farrell asked the initial question, but when he was stopped in his tracks and England attempted to recycle the ball, referee Romain Poite reached for his whistle and awarded England a penalty for an earlier offside against hooker Richard Hibbard. Wales clearly expected a penalty attempt from Farrell to follow, but Care had other

ideas. As the Welsh players fatally turned their backs on him and trudged to their own try line, the scrum-half took a quick tap and before anyone could react, let alone attempt a tackle, he was over the whitewash. Farrell's conversion sailed safely over and England were 7-0 in front.

Care's quick thinking and Wales' delayed reaction were to sum up the contest as the home side played with consistent ambition and precision. Three first-half penalties from the unerringly accurate boot of full-back Leigh Halfpenny kept Warren Gatland's stuttering side in touch, but Farrell landed two three-pointers of his own before Lancaster's team once again unlocked the Welsh defence.

A Wales lineout in their own 22 went awry and England pounced on the loose ball. Possession went smoothly through the hands in midfield before Jonny May cut back purposefully from the left touchline and stormed towards the line. He was eventually hauled down three metres short, but the ball reappeared invitingly from the resulting ruck and Care didn't miss a beat as he passed to Billy Twelvetrees on the blindside. Wales rushed out en masse to avert the danger, but the England centre saw the blitz coming and

Below left: Full-back Leigh Halfpenny scored all of Wales' points with six successful penalty attempts.

Below right: Scrum-half Danny Care scored England's first try at HQ to set up a 28–19 victory for the Red Rose.

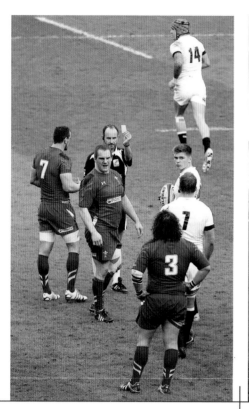

prodded a grubber kick behind them, which Luther Burrell was quickest to reach, outpacing Halfpenny for the touchdown to notch up his third try in only his fourth Test appearance. Farrell again made no mistake with the conversion and although Halfpenny was on target with two more penalties, it was 20–15 to the men in white as the teams disappeared down the Twickenham tunnel at half time.

The second 40 minutes saw points at a premium for both teams. Farrell's third successful penalty, in the 45th minute, was the first of the half and he added a fourth nine minutes later, only for Halfpenny to respond with his sixth successful kick of the contest. The England fly-half was then presented with his fifth penalty chance shortly afterwards, when Jonathan Davies was adjudged to have played the ball on the ground: his kick flew through the uprights and the Red Rose were 29–18 in front.

Surprisingly, there were no more scores at Twickenham. Wales temporarily went down to 14 men midway through the half when prop Gethin Jenkins was sin binned for not scrummaging straight, but England were

"It was a different type of game; the game against Ireland probably had a little bit more flow to it. But because of the significance of the game last year and obviously the pressure on the boys to deliver, in light of the World Cup in a year and a half's time and playing at Twickenham, the boys wanted to win this game and I'm delighted for them that they did."

Stuart Lancaster

Above left: **Wales prop Gethin Jenkins (middle) was shown a yellow card in the 53rd minute of the game at Twickenham.**

Above: **(left to right) Ben Morgan, Tom Wood and captain Chris Robshaw proudly display the Triple Crown trophy after beating Wales.**

unable to capitalize on his indiscipline and extend their 11-point advantage.

The closest Lancaster's side came to a third try came in the 73rd minute after a devastating counter attack from deep in their own half. Twelvetrees instigated the move, Burrell gave it impetus, and Jack Nowell kept it alive with an impudent flip behind his back to Courtney Lawes. England were closing menacingly on the Welsh line as Lawes offloaded to Burrell and the centre raced to the corner, only for his effort to be chalked off after he was tackled by Halfpenny and the TMO ruled his right foot had hit the touchline before he had grounded the ball.

It was to prove a minor disappointment rather than a major talking point, and when Poite blew for full time seven minutes later, Twickenham celebrated. England had beaten Wales to claim the Triple Crown and Lancaster's side had emulated at least one of the achievements of the famous class of 2003.

Equally significantly, the victory kept England in the hunt for the RBS 6 Nations title. France's 19-17 win over Scotland at Murrayfield, and Ireland's 46-7 demolition of the Italians in Dublin the previous day, meant the three teams were level on six points and it would be a three-way shootout for the trophy on the final weekend of the tournament. England's points difference may have been inferior to that of Ireland, but with Italy their final opponents in Rome in six days time, there was real hope that the team could yet become champions.

"We've tried to remove the fear of playing, and when you've got the courage of your convictions it generally pays off," Lancaster said after victory at HQ. "It's nice to get the win to put last year's result in Cardiff to bed. We lost fair and square on that day, but this was our day and we deserved to win.

"I was really proud of the team. They are a great set of lads who always want to play hard for each other and the shirt. It's a massive scalp [because] we all know what happened last year. We'd lost the last two times we'd played them [in the 6 Nations] and we needed some momentum back. We've now got ourselves back into contention and we're ticking along."

England 29	Wales 18
15 → Mike BROWN	15 → Leigh HALFPENNY
14 Jack NOWELL	14 Alex CUTHBERT
13 Luther BURRELL	13 Jonathan DAVIES
12 Billy TWELVETREES	12 Jamie ROBERTS
11 Jonny MAY	11 George NORTH
10 → Owen FARRELL	10 → Rhys PRIESTLAND
9 → Danny CARE	9 → Rhys WEBB
1 → Joe MARLER	1 → Gethin JENKINS
2 → Dylan HARTLEY	2 → Richard HIBBARD
3 → David WILSON	3 → Adam JONES
4 → Joe LAUNCHBURY	4 → Jake BALL
5 Courtney LAWES	5 Alun-Wyn JONES
6 → Tom WOOD	6 → Dan LYDIATE
7 Chris ROBSHAW (c)	7 Sam WARBURTON (c)
8 Ben MORGAN	8 Taulupe FALETAU

REPLACEMENTS	REPLACEMENTS
2 ← 16 Tom YOUNGS	2 ← 16 Ken OWENS
1 ← 17 Mako VUNIPOLA	1 ← 17 Paul JAMES
3 ← 18 Henry THOMAS	3 ← 18 Rhodri JONES
4 ← 19 Dave ATWOOD	4 ← 19 Andrew COOMBS
6 ← 20 Tom JOHNSON	6 ← 20 Justin TIPURIC
9 ← 21 Lee DICKSON	9 ← 21 Mike PHILLIPS
10 ← 22 George FORD	10 ← 22 Dan BIGGAR
15 ← 23 Alex GOODE	15 ← 23 Liam WILLIAMS

SCORES

SCORES

Tries: **Care** (4), **Burrell** (33)

Cons: **Farrell** (5, 34)

Pens: **Farrell** (18, 26, 45, 54, 58)

Pens: **Halfpenny** (8, 22, 30, 37, 40, 56)

England		Wales
38	Kicks from hand	31
137	Passes	31
141	Runs	127
596	Metres run with ball	430
50%	Possession	50%
52%	Territory	48%
6	Clean breaks	6
26	Defenders beaten	24
10	Offloads	10
82 from 86	Rucks won	92 from 95
3 from 4	Mauls won	2 from 3
12	Turnovers conceded	19
143/24	Tackles (made/missed)	131/26
86.0%	Tackling success rate	83.0%
7 won, 1 lost (87.5%)	Scrums on own feed	2 won, 0 lost (100.00%)
6 won, 1 lost (85.7%)	Lineouts on own throw	12 won, 2 lost (85.7%)
11 (0)	Penalties conceded (freekicks)	10 (0)
0/0	Yellow/red cards	1/0

Italy vs England

TRIES GALORE, BUT NO SILVERWARE

England Rugby

ITA 11

ENG 52

Date: 15 March 2014

Stadium: Stadio Olimpico, Rome

Attendance: 57,750

Referee: Pascal Gauzere (France)

The climax of the 15th instalment of the RBS 6 Nations was nothing if not tense, as England, Ireland and France still harboured dreams of being crowned champions. The Red Rose's fate was no longer in their own hands, leaving Stuart Lancaster's side with the task of defeating Italy in Rome before watching events unfold 700 miles away in the Stade de France later that evening.

Whatever the final scoreline against the *Azzurri* at the Stadio Olimpico, England knew they would be suspended in a state of ignorance for almost five hours after the final whistle had sounded in Rome. The fixture list had not been kind to England, and Lancaster's team were condemned to do battle in Italy with one hand tied behind their back.

The problem came with the kick-off times. England were billed in the early match of the championship's denouement, starting at 12.30pm, but title rivals France and Ireland were not scheduled to start hostilities in Paris until 5.00pm. The Red Rose would not know if they had done enough to become champions until long after the Stadio Olimpico was deserted.

Victory over the Italians was, of course, vital but, beyond that, England would be left with more questions than answers. Ireland were in pole position courtesy of their superior points difference (49) to England, but even an Irish victory in Paris would not guarantee them the trophy should it prove to be a narrow win. A deluge of points for Lancaster's team could still be enough to secure the silverware, while a French victory, coupled with a surprise English defeat, would leave Philippe

Left: **Mke Brown scored two of England's seven tries in their victory over Italy at the Stadio Olimpico.**

Above: **Wing Jack Nowell's score against the Italians in Rome was the first of his England career.**

Above right: **Mako Vunipola touches down to score England's fifth try in Rome.**

Saint-André's team with reason to celebrate.

Against this opaque backdrop, Lancaster could do no more than ensure England did their job in Rome, and although he had no fresh injuries to contend with, he was forced to bring in Mako Vunipola at loose head to replace Joe Marler when the Harlequins prop stayed at home for the birth of his first child. A fit-again Manu Tuilagi took Alex Goode's place among the replacements, and England were ready for the fray.

"It's irrelevant whether we kick off at the same time or later," Lancaster replied when asked about the staggering of the final round of matches. "We've still got to play well. I don't think it affects the outcome of a game knowing what you need to do. I don't think players or coaches think that way. You're that concentrated on your own detail, your own preparation.

"Rome is a fantastic opportunity for us to finish the 6 Nations on a high point. We want to put in a performance that backs up the previous performances. That is a big motivation for the players."

Rome was bathed in March sunshine for the match and, although the home side took the lead through a Luciano Orquera penalty after only six minutes, England's victory was never in doubt once Mike Brown raced over in the 12th minute for the first of the visitors' seven tries. Luther Burrell burst through an Italian tackle to create the space and Brown was on hand to take the offload, outpacing both Luke McLean and Michele Campagnaro in the foot race to the line that ensued.

A Mako Vunipola trundle followed by thrusts from Ben Morgan and Danny Care provided the platform for the second try, scored by Owen Farrell, while Brown completed a double three minutes before half time, this time outsprinting *Azzurri* wing Angelo Esposito to leave the Red Rose 24–6 to the good at the break.

It was now a matter of how many points England could amass in the Stadio Olimpico, but they had to wait for 12 minutes into the second half before the fourth try came. Morgan flicked the ball through his legs to Care from the base of an attacking scrum. The scrum-half fed Farrell, who in turn found Brown and, rather than selfishly look for his hat-trick, the full-back set up Jack Nowell from short range for the first try of the Exeter flyer's fledgling international career.

Vunipola took England further ahead on the hour. Courtney Lawes, pressed into emergency service at scrum-half, passed to Twelvetrees, who got behind an increasingly tired Italian defence before feeding Vunipola, who strolled unopposed under the posts. Lancaster emptied his bench, and Tuilagi gate-crashed the party with England's sixth try when he took a short pass from Farrell in midfield and contemptuously swatted away two *Azzurri* tacklers to crash over.

The procession was briefly interrupted in the 68th minute, when wing Leonardo Sarto intercepted Joe Launchbury's pass to Vunipola and sped over for a consolation score for the home side, but England had the final word when replacement George Ford, making only his second Test appearance, sold an extravagant dummy and danced through the Italian defence in the last minute before presenting skipper Chris Robshaw with a gift-wrapped scoring opportunity. Farrell made it a superb seven successful conversions from seven attempts and England were 52–11 winners.

The half-century of points was reward for another magnificent performance from Lancaster's team, but it would count for little if the result in Paris did not go their way.

In the end, it was agonizingly close. After an hour in the Stade de France, *Les Bleus* trailed the Irish 22–13, but when hooker Dimitri Szarzewski went over with 17 minutes remaining and Maxime Machenaud converted, France were just two points adrift.

Roared on by a vociferous Parisian crowd, France unleashed wave after wave of attack in search of the winning score, and they seemed to have found it in the 78th minute when No.8 Damien Chouly went over in the corner – only for the TMO to rule out his effort for a forward pass by Vincent Debaty.

The score would have given England the championship title, but Ireland held on for

a 22–20 win, only their second triumph in Paris in 42 years. The result saw England and Ireland both finish the campaign with eight points, but Joe Schmidt's team took the title courtesy of a positive points difference of 83 compared to the Red Rose's 73. Lancaster's team had come within a whisker of the title, but ultimately had to satisfy themselves with the Triple Crown and runners-up spot in the final table.

"We always knew this was going to be one of the tightest 6 Nations and go down to the wire, but credit to Ireland," the England head coach said after news of Ireland's win in France filtered through.

"Our intent to attack, the quality of our defence and set piece has been excellent. We are in good shape going forward.

"I am very proud of what we have achieved over the tournament, both in how this young group has developed and also our intent to play attacking rugby. We have fielded 28 players, but it's been a whole squad effort from players, coaches and management.

"I'd also include the supporters in that, both at Twickenham and away, because they have been brilliant and have bought into what we are trying to achieve."

Opposite: **Manu Tuilagi's try in the Stadio Olimpico was his 11th for the Red Rose in his 23rd Test match appearance.**

Left: **England captain Chris Robshaw underlined England's dominance with a try in the final minute of the game in Rome.**

Italy 11	England 52
15 Luke **McLEAN**	15 Mike **BROWN**
14 Angelo **ESPOSITO**	14 Jack **NOWELL**
13 Michele **CAMPAGNARO**	13 → Luther **BURRELL**
12 → Gonzalo **GARCIA**	12 → Billy **TWELVETREES**
11 Leonardo **SARTO**	11 Jonny **MAY**
10 → Luciano **ORQUERA**	10 Owen **FARRELL**
9 → Tito **TEBALDI**	9 → Danny **CARE**
1 → Matias **AGUERO**	1 → Mako **VUNIPOLA**
2 Leonardo **GHIRALDINI**	2 Dylan **HARTLEY**
3 → Lorenzo **CITTADINI**	3 David **WILSON**
4 Quintin **GELDENHUYS**	4 → Joe **LAUNCHBURY**
5 Marco **BORTOLAMI**	5 Courtney **LAWES**
6 → Joshua **FURNO**	6 → Tom **WOOD**
7 Robert **Barbieri**	7 Chris **ROBSHAW** (c)
8 Sergio **PARISSE** (c)	8 Ben **MORGAN**

REPLACEMENTS	REPLACEMENTS
16 Davide **GIAZZON**	2 ← 16 Tom **YOUNGS**
1 ← 17 Michele **RIZZO**	1 ← 17 Matt **MULLAN**
3 ← 18 Alberto **DE MARCHI**	3 ← 18 Henry **THOMAS**
20 ← 19 George Fabio **BIAGI**	4 ← 19 Dave **ATWOOD**
6 ← 20 Paul **DERBYSHIRE**	6 ← 20 Tom **JOHNSON**
9 ← 21 Edoardo **GORI**	9 ← 21 Lee **DICKSON**
10 ← 22 Tomasso **ALLAN**	12 ← 22 George **FORD**
12 ← 23 Andrea **MASI**	13 ← 23 Manusamoa **TUILAGI**

SCORES

Try: **Sarto** (68)

Pens: **Orquera** (6, 22)

SCORES

Tries: **Brown** (12, 37), **Farrell** (31), **Nowell** (52), **Vunipola** (60), **Tuilagi** (67), **Robshaw** (80)

Cons: **Farrell** (13, 32, 39, 53, 61, 67, 80)

Pen: **Farrell** (10)

Italy		England
13	Kicks from hand	17
97	Passes	213
81	Runs	133
273	Metres run with ball	524
39%	Possession	61%
32%	Territory	68%
4	Clean breaks	12
9	Defenders beaten	29
9	Offloads	19
51 from 57	Rucks won	86 from 92
0 from 1	Mauls won	7 from 9
20	Turnovers conceded	21
122/29	Tackles (made/missed)	76/9
81.0%	Tackling success rate	89.0%
7 won, 4 lost (63.6%)	Scrums on own feed	5 won, 0 lost (100.00%)
8 won, 4 lost (66.7%)	Lineouts on own throw	18 won, 1 lost (94.7%)
14 (0)	Penalties conceded (freekicks)	9 (1)
1/0	Yellow/red cards	0/0

"We have produced a big scoreline on the back of a Sunday game against Wales – opponents who emotionally and physically took a lot out of the players – with a team that has an average age of 24. We haven't got everything right in every game, but when you put everything into perspective we have made great progress."

Stuart Lancaster

IN PROFILE:

Chris Robshaw

The inspirational focal point for the Red Rose's recent resurgence as a force on the world stage, the Harlequins flanker has had to overcome a precipitous learning curve since he was abruptly thrust into the spotlight after his appointment as England captain.

England Rugby

Position: **Flanker**

Age: **28**

Height: **1.88m**

Weight: **110kg**

Caps: **32**

It was in early 2012 that Stuart Lancaster turned to Chris Robshaw and asked him to help rebuild the England team in the wake of the ill-fated World Cup campaign in New Zealand. The two men were already acquainted with one another having worked together with the England Saxons, and Lancaster was convinced a reprisal of their relationship at senior level was key to his plans.

To say that Robshaw was dropped in at the deep end would be an understatement. The flanker had experienced just 53 fleeting minutes of Test rugby in 2009 before he led out the Red Rose for the Calcutta Cup clash against Scotland at Murrayfield, and there were those who questioned the interim coach's wisdom.

The dissenting voices are conspicuous by their absence today, however. England battled to victory that day in Edinburgh, and the captain has galvanized his team with pride, bravery and a series of outstanding individual performances ever since. New Zealand, Australia, Wales, France and Ireland have all fallen to the Red Rose during Robshaw's impressive reign and, as he has grown into the role, England have risen inexorably back up the IRB world rankings.

It's been a frenetic ride since he took the armband, but throughout it all Robshaw has radiated a disarming calm both in the face of media scrutiny and the bruising hits of opposition forwards aiming to knock him over.

"When you sign up for the job of England captain you know that there will be good days and some tough days," he said. "You never fully master the art of captaincy, *but* I've always said it's not about who you are but what you do, and I've always got to make sure

that I perform as a player first. The captaincy is not a one-man job. There are a number of generals on the pitch and a lot of leaders in the squad who help to drive it."

A significant, but largely overlooked, milestone in his captaincy came against Wales at Twickenham in the 2014 RBS 6 Nations. The post-match post mortems were predictably dominated by England's dominance in a 28–19 victory that secured the Triple Crown, but what was almost forgotten was the fact that it was Robshaw's 23rd Test at the helm, surpassing Lawrence Dallaglio's tally of 22 games as captain. Only Will Carling and Martin Johnson have now skippered England in more Tests matches.

> "When you sign up for the job of England captain you know that there will be good days and some tough days,"
>
> ## Chris Robshaw

After missing out on selection for the 2011 World Cup in New Zealand, despite being named in the provisional squad, the 2015 tournament will be Robshaw's first on the game's biggest stage. Only Carling before him has enjoyed the opportunity of leading England into a World Cup on home soil, progressing all the way to final, while Johnson is the only Englishman to have lifted the Webb Ellis Cup. Robshaw would dearly love to emulate both men in 2015 in one fell swoop.

Opposite: Chris Robshaw has led from the front since taking on the England captaincy and he scored his second international try in the defeat of Italy in Rome in 2014.

England in New Zealand, summer 2014

Few teams venture into the All Blacks' backyard and emerge victorious. Playing in New Zealand is the ultimate test, and as England embarked on the latest phase of their develpment, they were under no illusions they were about to enter the lion's den. England teams had dared to tread in New Zealand on a dozen occasions since their first visit to Auckland in 1963 and only twice had the Red Rose emerged victorious. Stuart Lancaster's tourists would be joining elite company indeed if they were able to register a win in the three-Test series against the defending world champions. First, though, they would face the Barbarians at Twickenham.

England line up to face the New Zealand All Blacks as they perform the Haka before the second Test at Forsyth-Barr Stadium, Dunedin.

England XV vs The Barbarians

England
Rugby

BARBARIANS AT THE TWICKENHAM GATES

It may have been an unfamiliar England XV that took to the Twickenham pitch at the start of June to face the Baa-Baas, but a new generation of Red Rose players acquitted themselves admirably. The non-cap match was ultimately lost, but not before fledgling reputations had been enhanced and the 50,000-strong crowd had witnessed an eight-try thriller.

England 29
Barbarians 39

Date: **1 June 2014**
Stadium: **Twickenham Stadium, London**
Attendance: **50,498**
Referee: **Mathieu Raynal (France)**

The contrast in experience between the two teams that did battle at HQ could not have been more stark. The Barbarians XV, coached by former England No.8 Dean Ryan, boasted more than 700 Test caps in their ranks, and could call on such iconic names as Joe Rokocoko, Juan Martin Hernandez and François Trinh-Duc.

England were compelled to select from more modest resources. With Stuart Lancaster and an initial 30-man squad already departed for the tour of New Zealand and the Premiership final the previous day ruling Northampton and Saracens players out of contention, the coaching duo of Joe Lydon and Jon Callard had difficult selection choices to make.

Perhaps inevitably, they opted for youth. Leicester second row Graham Kitchener was named captain and although they were able to call on three full internationals in the shape of centre Jonathan Joseph, wing Charlie Sharples and scrum-half Joe Simpson, their new-look side was nothing if not experimental.

The 14th meeting between England and the Baa-Baas began at a breathless pace, but it was not until the 12th minute that the first points were scored, and they went to England. A sniping run from Simpson deep in the opposition 22 was the catalyst and when he was brought down, Exeter Chiefs No.8 Dave Ewers was on hand to pick up and barge his way through two tacklers and over from two metres.

Left: **Fraser Balmain of England shakes hands with Julien Brugnaut of the Barbarians at the end of the match.**

Fly-half Henry Slade added the conversion, and the home side were up and running.

Adhering to the Barbarians long and proud tradition of playing expansive, attacking rugby, the class of 2014 hit back, and after a mercurial exchange of passes between Kiwi centres Benson Stanley and Rene Ranger, the former squeezed over the line in the 18th minute. England, however, were unfazed.

They scored their second try through Sharples, who collected Ollie Devoto's intelligent grubber kick before the defence could turn and cover, and while the Baa-Baas replied with a well-worked score from fullback Hernandez, England led their illustrious opponents 18–14 at half time.

The first score of the second period went to the visitors, when Georgia back-rower Mamuka Gorgodze burst from the base of an attacking scrum and bulldozed his way over the line. French referee Mathieu Raynal initially declined to award the try, but the TMO was called into action and replays confirmed that the No.8 had stretched sufficiently to touch down.

Once again England refused to wilt, and they were back in contention midway through the half. A series of penetrating phases took them into the Baa-Baas 22, but when the ball found its way to Slade there seemed no room for manoeuvre on the right touchline. The young Exeter 10 was determined to score, wriggling his way through three tackles before reaching desperately for the line. Once again the TMO was in play and once again he deemed a try had been scored. Slade may have been unable to add the two additional points, but England were now only 24–23 adrift.

The result was in the balance with a quarter of the match remaining, but it was the Baa-Baas' greater firepower that eventually told, as former All Black wing Hosea Gear showed his international class with the two late tries that killed off England's challenge and handed the Barbarians an entertaining 39–29 victory.

The match undoubtedly proved a positive experience for uncapped Harlequins prop Kyle Sinckler. The day after the Baa-Baas game, Lancaster named 16 more players to join the squad that had already decamped to New Zealand, and 21-year-old Sinckler was rewarded for his efforts at Twickenham with a place in the tour party.

England 29		Barbarians 39	
15	Eliot DALY	15	Juan Martin HERNANDEZ
14	Semesa ROKODUGUNI	14	Joe ROKOCOKO
13 →	Jonathan JOSEPH	13 →	Rene RANGER
12	Sam HILL	12	Benson STANLEY
11 →	Charlie SHARPLES	11	Hosea GEAR
10	Henry SLADE	10 →	Brock JAMES
9 →	Joe SIMPSON	9 →	Jimmy COWAN
1 →	Ross HARRISON	1 →	Sona TAUMALOLO
2 →	Rob BUCHANAN	2 →	Ti'i PAULO
3 →	Kyle SINCKLER	3 →	Davit KUBRIASHVILI
4 →	Michael PATERSON	4 →	Donncha O'CALLAGHAN
5	Graham KITCHENER	5	Juandre KRUGER
6 →	Jamie GIBSON	6	Juan Manuel LEGUIZAMON
7	Luke WALLACE	7 →	Alexandre LAPANDRY
8	Dave EWERS	8	Mamuka GORGODZE

REPLACEMENTS		REPLACEMENTS	
2 ←	16 Tommy TAYLOR	2 ←	16 Andrew HORE
1 ←	17 Fraser BALMAIN	1 ←	17 Julien BRUGNAUT
3 ←	18 Will COLLIER	3 ←	18 Nahuel LOBO
4 ←	19 Charlie MATTHEWS	7 ←	19 Roger WILSON
6 ←	20 James GASKELL	4 ←	20 Joe TEKORI
9 ←	21 Dan ROBSON	9 ←	21 Tomas CUBELLI
13 ←	22 Ollie DEVOTO	10 ←	22 François TRINH-DUC
11 ←	23 Rob MILLER	13 ←	23 Anthony TUITAVAKE

SCORES

Tries: Ewers (11), Sharples (23), Slade (55)

Con: Slade (13)

Pens: Daly (21), Slade (36, 61, 67)

SCORES

Tries: Stanley (17), Hernandez (26), Gorgodze (45), Gear (63, 76)

Cons: James (18, 28, 46), Trinh-Duc (64)

Pens: James (51), Trinh-Duc (58)

England supporters could now focus their thoughts on the three Tests that lay in wait south of the equator and their team's prospects of downing the All Blacks in their own country. The first Test in Auckland was just five days away, and the clock was ticking.

"Things are very promising for England. Some 60 to 70 players are being used this month [by England] ahead of the World Cup and we did well today against a far more experienced side."

Jon Callard

New Zealand vs England

THE FIRST TEST

The record books did not make for encouraging reading as England braced themselves for battle in Auckland. The All Blacks had not lost at Eden Park in 20 years, an incredible 31-match winning sequence, and they had last suffered a Test defeat anywhere on home soil in 2009. Stuart Lancaster's depleted side were dismissed as sacrificial lambs by certain sections of the media, but if the newspapers were downbeat about the tourists' prospects, the England players had evidently not been reading them.

England Rugby

NZL 20
ENG 15

Date: **7 June 2014**
Stadium: **Eden Park, Auckland**
Attendance: **48,000**
Referee: **Nigel Owens (Wales)**

The modern rugby calendar is an increasingly complicated and overloaded beast. The players' workload becomes more onerous each season, and as Lancaster prepared his troops for the first Test against New Zealand, the England head coach would have been forgiven for bemoaning the nightmare of fixture congestion.

Characteristically, he declined to rage against the injustice, but the fact remained that with the first Test in Auckland scheduled for just seven days after the Premiership final between Northampton and Saracens at Twickenham, Lancaster was unable to call on the services of 12 leading internationals from the two best club sides in England. The players had already flown into New Zealand, but they were tired and bruised and the coach

Left: **Gloucester fly-half Freddie Burns won his fourth cap for England in the first Test against New Zealand at Eden Park.**

Above: **All Black fly-half Aaron Cruden contributed 15 points with the boot in Auckland.**

Above right: **Wing Marland Yarde was sent to the sin bin in the 69th minute of England's narrow defeat to the All Blacks.**

had decided the unavoidably late arrivals would not be considered for selection for the opening match of the tour.

England were still able to name a match-day 23 that boasted 376 caps between them. The New Zealand team may have had 968 caps on their collective CV, but the Red Rose were certainly no international novices, despite missing eight of the players who had started in the victory over Italy in Rome in March.

The pre-match debate was whether Freddie Burns or Danny Cipriani would get the nod for the fly-half berth temporarily vacated by Owen Farrell. Lancaster opted for Burns as his first-choice 10, while Ben Youngs replaced the injured Danny Care at nine to complete a new-look half-back pairing. The uncapped duo of Worcester full-back Chris Pennell and Harlequins hooker Joe Gray were named on the bench.

"This is a big opportunity for me," Burns admitted after the team was announced. "I'm really excited to get out there and we have a good bunch of boys in the team. We've trained exceptionally well and we're ready for Saturday.

"To play the All Blacks over here at Eden Park is something that you can't let daunt you. You've just got to get excited about it and go out there and have a go. We've been in camp for two weeks now already, so are

champing at the bit to get out there and really get stuck in."

The last time England had really got stuck into the All Blacks in New Zealand was in 2003, when Clive Woodward's side recorded a famous 15–13 victory in Wellington, and Lancaster's 2014 vintage were to come agonizingly close to emulating their feat.

The visitors began with a tangible bang in Auckland when captain Chris Robshaw burst through the first-up Kiwi defence as early as the second minute and galloped clear. James Haskell raced up in support, but was tugged back off the ball by Ma'a Nonu and when the move broke down, Welsh referee Nigel Owens retrospectively awarded a penalty. The All Black centre was lucky not to be despatched to the sin bin for his cynical offence, and England had to be content with a 3–0 lead as Burns stepped up to kick the penalty.

New Zealand eased themselves into the game with an Aaron Cruden penalty after England had strayed offside, but the Red Rose went 9–3 up with two further Burns kicks.

His first penalty opportunity was earned after Haskell, Kyle Eastmond, who was hauled down just short by Israel Dagg, and Manu Tuilagi had made inroads, while the second was awarded in the 21st minute after the All Black front row was penalized for not pushing straight at a scrum.

Left: **Conrad Smith scored the winning try for New Zealand three minutes from time in the first Test.**

At this stage, England had the world champions on the back foot, but the Kiwis called on their collective and considerable experience to steady the ship and they clawed their way back into contention with two more Cruden penalties.

The two teams went into the dressing room at half time locked at 9–9, but it was so nearly England who held the advantage after a pulsating break from the base of the scrum from inside his own 22 by No.8 Ben Morgan. Eastmond provided a timely option as the defence reorganized, but with the line seemingly at England's mercy, his pass to Mike Brown went astray and the chance was gone.

The two teams continued to attack and counter attack throughout the second 40 minutes, as first the tourists and then the Kiwis asserted themselves. England went 12–9 ahead after a chip and chase earned them a penalty, which Burns calmly accepted, but the All Blacks were on terms again three minutes later courtesy of Cruden's boot.

What proved to be the pivotal moment of an absorbing encounter came in the 70th minute. New Zealand worked space for Brodie Retallick and as the second row galloped past the first line of defence, Marland Yarde was forced to come flying off his wing and make the hit. It decisively halted the attack but, as

the New Zealand forwards piled into the ruck, Yarde was punished for not rolling away and was shown a yellow card. Cruden made no mistake with the ensuing penalty. Trailing 15–12, England were forced to play the rest of the match with 14 men.

The introduction of Cipriani from the bench, winning his eighth cap nearly four years after his seventh, gave the visitors renewed impetus, and it was his scything midfield break that earned England their fifth penalty. The Sale fly-half accepted the three points on offer and, with seven minutes remaining, it was all square at 15–15.

A historic victory was still within England's grasp, but hope turned to heartbreak just

"We got there in the end, but we need to be a lot better going into the second Test and we expect England to be better."

Richie McCaw

Opposite: **Henry Thomas (left) and Marland Yarde reflect on England's late loss at Eden Park**

two minutes from time when the All Blacks won another penalty. Cruden declined to take a shot at goal and took the quick tap, and although the depleted Red Rose repelled close-range thrusts from Jerome Kaino and Wyatt Crockett, the ball was recycled to Ben Smith on the blindside and his instinctive first-time pass found Conrad Smith. Prop Joe Marler desperately tried to get across, but he was too late to stop the Kiwi centre, who dived over at the corner for what turned out to be the match-winning try.

The match finished 20–15 in New Zealand's favour and England's titanic effort went unrewarded. The Kiwi's formidable winning run at Eden Park was extended to 32 games, but the reigning world champions had been given a significant scare.

"To lose the game in that way was immensely frustrating," admitted England forwards coach Graham Rowntree. "We challenged the forward pack to take their game to the next level and they did that. There were noble performances from Rob Webber, who hasn't played much rugby, and I thought he was exceptional today, as was Ben Morgan, who had his best performance in an England shirt."

England were 1–0 down in the three-match series, but with the second Test in Dunedin just seven days away, Lancaster and his squad left Auckland with the belief they were capable of toppling the All Blacks in the Forysth-Barr Stadium to level the series.

New Zealand 20	England 15
15 → Israel DAGG	15 Mike BROWN
14 Ben SMITH	14 Marland YARDE
13 Conrad SMITH	13 Manusamoa TUILAGI
12 → Ma'a NONU	12 Kyle EASTMOND
11 Cory JANE	11 → Jonny MAY
10 Aaron CRUDEN	10 → Freddie BURNS
9 → Aaron SMITH	9 Ben YOUNGS
1 → Tony WOODCOCK	1 Joe MARLER
2 → Dane COLES	2 → Rob WEBBER
3 → Owen FRANKS	3 David WILSON
4 Brodie RETALLICK	4 Joe LAUNCHBURY
5 Sam WHITELOCK	5 Geoff PARLING
6 → Liam MESSAM	6 → James HASKELL
7 Richie McCAW (c)	7 Chris ROBSHAW (c)
8 Jerome KAINO	8 Ben MORGAN

REPLACEMENTS	REPLACEMENTS
2 ← 16 Keven MEALAMU	2 ← 16 Joe GRAY
1 ← 17 Wyatt CROCKETT	17 Matt MULLAN
3 ← 18 Charlie FAUMUINA	3 ← 18 Henry THOMAS
19 Patrick TUIPULOTU	4 ← 19 Dave ATWOOD
6 ← 20 Victor VITO	6 ← 20 Tom JOHNSON
9 ← 21 TJ PERENARA	9 ← 21 Lee DICKSON
15 ← 22 Beauden BARRETT	10 ← 22 Danny CIPRIANI
12 ← 23 Malakai FEKITOA	11 ← 23 Chris PENNELL

SCORES

Try: CG Smith (77)

Pens: Cruden (9, 24, 38, 66, 70)

SCORES

Pens: Burns (2, 18, 21, 63), Cipriani (73)

34	Kicks from hand	25
109	Passes	146
83	Runs	91
311	Metres run with ball	361
44%	Possession	56%
44%	Territory	56%
5	Clean breaks	8
13	Defenders beaten	22
4	Offloads	8
52 from 53	Rucks won	71 from 75
4 from 5	Mauls won	5 from 6
12	Turnovers conceded	18
105/22	Tackles (made/missed)	82/13
83.0%	Tackling success rate	86.0%
11 won, 1 lost (91.7%)	Scrums on own feed	6 won, 0 lost (100.0%)
9 won, 1 lost (90.0%)	Lineouts on own throw	13 won, 0 lost (100.0%)
7 (1)	Penalties conceded (freekicks)	8 (2)
1/0	Yellow/red cards	1/0

New Zealand vs England

THE SECOND TEST

Perhaps it was a blessing that England had only a week to recover from their agony in Auckland. Time may be the great healer, but the proximity of the second Test meant that the squad was not afforded a period of prolonged introspection. Stuart Lancaster's troops may have lost the opening battle, but the war was far from over – and with the heavy artillery from Northampton Saints and Saracens ready for action, the tourists had reason enough for hope.

NZL 28

ENG 27

Date: 14 June 2014
Stadium: Forsyth-Barr
Stadium, Dunedin
Attendance: 28,470
Referee: Jaco Peyper
(South Africa)

It was a determinedly upbeat Lancaster who faced the media before the second Test in Dunedin. The England head coach was the epitome of positivity, and whatever his thoughts behind closed doors may have been, he refused to accept that his side had squandered their best chance of beating the All Blacks at Eden Park.

The announcement of his team for the game at the Forysth-Barr Stadium was one of the most eagerly anticipated of his England reign. Although he now had a full deck to play with, Lancaster resisted the temptation to parachute all of the late arrivals straight into his starting XV.

The headline news was his decision to switch Manu Tuilagi from the midfield to the right wing. To accommodate the Welford Road wrecking ball, Marland Yarde moved to the left wing and Jonny May dropped out of the match-day 23 altogether. A new-look midfield saw the fit-again Billy Twelvetrees

Below: Wing Marland Yarde powered his way over for the first try of the second Test against New Zealand in Dunedin.

Above: **All Black centre Ma'a Nonu was one of the home side's three try-scorers against England in the Forsyth-Barr Stadium.**

Above right: **Fly-half Owen Farrell kicked 12 points for the Red Rose in Dunedin after his recall to the team.**

reunited with Luther Burrell, while there was also a familiar look to the half-backs as Danny Care and Owen Farrell were reinstated to replace Ben Youngs and Freddie Burns.

There was only a slight readjustment to the forwards, with Tom Wood in for James Haskell at blindside the only change to a pack that had made significant inroads against the Kiwis in the first Test. On the bench, uncapped tight-head Kieran Brookes was preferred to Henry Thomas, while Dylan Hartley, Courtney Lawes and Billy Vunipola all bolstered Lancaster's options.

"It's a 23-man squad, and certainly the [players on the] bench and the impact they make from the bench, will be critical in the game," Lancaster said. "It's an 80-minute game against the All Blacks, and to have those calibre of men coming on in the second half I think will lift our performance.

"In the back line I always wanted a balance of pace, power, footballers and people who can distribute as well. We need to find out about these players. I'd rather find out now than 12 months from the World Cup and it's an exciting back line, there's no doubt about it."

England started brightly in Dunedin, and the pack's muscular efforts were rewarded as early as the second minute when Farrell kicked a penalty, a score that took England

past 500 points against the All Blacks since the teams met for the first time in 1905.

They nearly extended their lead minutes later, when Joe Launchbury charged down Aaron Smith's box kick, collected the bouncing ball and galloped towards the line. His beautifully timed inside pass to Wood took England closer and the flanker found Rob Webber in support, only for the hooker to be stopped inches short of the line.

The visitors were firmly on top in the early exchanges and moved 10–0 in front in the seventh minute following a Yarde try. Chris Robshaw took an attacking lineout ball, Care accepted possession and fed the onrushing wing inside the Kiwi 22. There didn't appear to be a hole in the New Zealand defence, but Yarde exploded through Richie McCaw, Aaron Cruden and Jerome Kaino's attempted tackles for the score. Farrell knocked over the conversion and England were flying.

A Cruden penalty cut the deficit, but still the tourists continued to dominate and should have gone it at half time further ahead. A 39th-minute attack from the All Blacks broke down, and when the ball bobbled mischievously on the deck, Tuilagi was the first to react, collected possession and brushed off Cruden's tackle. The Leicester Tiger sprinted from inside his own 22 deep into New Zealand territory, but was hauled

down by full-back Ben Smith before he could offload to Mike Brown. To add insult to injury, there was enough time remaining for the Kiwis to win a penalty, which Cruden landed. England had to be satisfied with a 10–6 lead at the break, but they knew it could – and perhaps should – have been better.

New Zealand emerged chastened for the second half in the Forysth-Barr Stadium and bombarded England for the first 20 minutes of the second period. The Red Rose made tackle after tackle, but the All Blacks breached the unrelenting defence three times.

An incisive counter-attack sent Ben Smith over in the 43rd minute after good work from Cruden and Julian Savea, and six minutes later it was Savea's turn to score after a typically abrasive thrust from Ma'a Nonu. The try put the home side 18–13 ahead, and their cause was significantly furthered after 58 minutes when referee Jaco Peyper showed Farrell a yellow card for not releasing the ball. New Zealand stretched further ahead midway through the half when Nonu eluded the grasp of Yarde and Burrell after Conrad Smith's break. Substitute Beauden Barrett added the two points and England were 28–13 adrift.

The fightback that ensued was as spectacular as it was, just, too late. The Red Rose's first counter punch came in the 70th minute as the forwards rumbled towards the

New Zealand line. Joe Marler was pressed into service as a stand-in scrum-half and the prop's crisp pass found Farrell. The fly-half went left and fed Twelvetrees, who looked up and span a long pass to Brown. The full-back cut back inside and burst through Ben Smith's tackle, but Cory Jane enveloped him as the two players crashed over the line together. Peyper consulted the TMO to confirm whether Brown had successfully grounded the ball and, after a nervous minute for England, the try was awarded. Farrell kicked the conversion and the tourists were now only eight points in arrears.

A characteristically direct charge from Tuilagi created England's third try. The England powerhouse took Wood's pass and sucked in two All Black tacklers in open field before offloading to Brown. The full-back raced down the touchline and when Ben Smith made the decision to move up and make the tackle, Brown found substitute Chris Ashton in eager support and the Saracens wing had an unfettered route to the line, touching down exuberantly beneath the posts. The immaculate Farrell was on target with his third conversion of the match, and the score was now 28–27 to the Kiwis.

Sadly, however, there was to be no fairytale climax for Lancaster's team, as Farrell's kick was the final play of the match. As Peyper

Above: **Mike Brown's fifth international try gave England hope of a famous victory in the second Test in Dunedin.**

Opposite: **England were left heartbroken by their one-point defeat in the Forsyth-Barr Stadium against the world champions.**

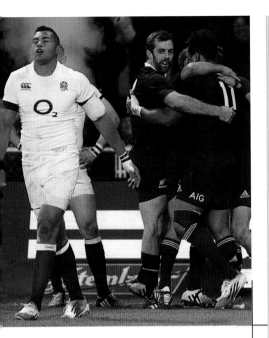

blew for full time, England had lost by a single point.

"We've come a long way in the past few weeks and we'll continue to get better," captain Robshaw said after the game. "We just lost a bit of control early in that second half. We just couldn't get hold of the ball really. We showed glimpses, we finished really strongly, we started really strongly, it was just that middle bit.

"It's a result-based industry and, unfortunately, we've had two losses and lost the series. But we've got another match to come next week, and we're going to come out fighting again."

New Zealand 28 | England 27

New Zealand 28	England 27
15 Ben SMITH	15 Mike BROWN
14 Cory JANE	14 Manusamoa TUILAGI
13 Conrad SMITH	13 → Luther BURRELL
12 Ma'a NONU	12 Billy TWELVETREES
11 Julian SAVEA	11 Marland YARDE
10 → Aaron CRUDEN	10 Owen FARRELL
9 → Aaron SMITH	9 → Danny CARE
1 → Tony WOODCOCK	1 → Joe MARLER
2 Dane COLES	2 → Rob WEBBER
3 Owen FRANKS	3 → David WILSON
4 → Brodie RETALLICK	4 → Joe LAUNCHBURY
5 Sam WHITELOCK	5 Geoff PARLING
6 → Liam MESSAM	6 Tom WOOD
7 Richie McCAW (c)	7 Chris ROBSHAW (c)
8 Jerome KAINO	8 → Ben MORGAN

REPLACEMENTS	REPLACEMENTS
2 ← 16 Keven MEALAMU	2 16 Dylan HARTLEY
1 ← 17 Wyatt CROCKETT	1 17 Matt MULLAN
3 ← 18 Charlie FAUMUINA	3 18 Kieran BROOKES
4 ← 19 Patrick TUIPULOTU	4 ← 19 Courtney LAWES
6 ← 20 Victor VITO	8 20 Billy VUNIPOLA
9 ← 21 TJ PERENARA	9 21 Ben YOUNGS
10 ← 22 Beauden BARRETT	22 Freddie BURNS
23 Malakai FEKITOA	13 ← 23 Chris ASHTON

SCORES

Tries: BR Smith (43), Savea (49), Nonu (63)
Cons: Cruden (44), Barrett (65)
Pens: Cruden (11, 40), Barrett (59)

SCORES

Tries: Yarde (7), Brown (71), Ashton (80)
Cons: Farrell (8, 71, 80)
Pens: Farrell (2, 47)

26	Kicks from hand	27
200	Passes	142
135	Runs	91
567	Metres run with ball	358
61%	Possession	39%
60%	Territory	40%
11	Clean breaks	7
31	Defenders beaten	11
11	Offloads	17
93 from 96	Rucks won	53 from 59
4 from 5	Mauls won	10 from 10
20	Turnovers conceded	19
74/11	Tackles (made/missed)	136/31
87.0%	Tackling success rate	81.0%
8 won, 2 lost (80.0%)	Scrums on own feed	4 won, 0 lost (100.0%)
10 won, 0 lost (100.0%)	Lineouts on own throw	12 won, 3 lost (80.0%)
9 (1)	Penalties conceded (freekicks)	7 (0)
0/0	Yellow/red cards	1/0

Crusaders vs England

MIDWEEK MATCH

England Rugby

Crusaders 7
England 38

Date: 17 June 2014
Stadium: AMI Stadium,
Christchurch
Attendance: 17,500
Referee: Nigel Owens
(Wales)

Two defeats in the first two Tests had left England bloodied but unbowed, and with a midweek game against the Crusaders in Christchurch on the immediate horizon, the tourists sensed the opportunity to open their tour account. It would be a completely overhauled English XV tasked by Stuart Lancaster to secure a morale-boosting victory over the Super Rugby heavyweights and it accomplished the mission with no shortage of style.

Midweek fixtures have become something of an endangered species in the modern game. Tours nowadays tend to focus on Tests, so it was a refreshing anomaly that England agreed to face the Crusaders at the AMI Stadium ahead of the third and final Test against the All Blacks. With a large squad at his disposal, Lancaster certainly had the resources for the game.

Unsurprisingly, none of the starting XV or replacements from the second Test defeat in Dunedin were named in the team as the head coach rung the changes. Leicester second row Ed Slater was given the captain's armband, and he was joined in the line-up by three other uncapped players, Gloucester centre Henry Trinder, Bath wing Anthony Watson and Northampton prop Alex Waller.

The Crusaders, the seven-time Super Rugby champions, may have been deprived of ten All Black squad members, but coach Todd Blackadder was still able to name a strong squad for the game that included six players with caps for the Kiwis.

The stage was set for what promised to be an entertaining adjunct to the unfolding Test series, and the Christchurch clash did not disappoint as England's second string cut loose to score six tries in a 38–7 triumph.

The visitors set the tone early and went over the whitewash in the very first minute. The England forwards drove purposefully from a lineout and the ball was worked towards Danny Cipriani. The fly-half made the initial break and as Crusaders full-back Tom Taylor closed, found Joe Gray. The hooker crashed over, Cipriani converted and England had raced into a 7–0 advantage.

There was no let-up in intensity and, five

Below left: **Bath wing Anthony Watson was one of England's six different try-scorers against the Crusaders.**

Below: **Flanker Matt Kvesic looks to offload to a team-mate before the ball is tackled by Crusaders' Andy Ellis (right).**

minutes later, England scored their second try. Alex Goode chipped to the corner and Ben Foden, playing on the right wing rather than at full-back, beat Johnny McNicholl to the ball for the touchdown. Cipriani's conversion may have sailed wide, but the tourists' lead was now up to 12 points.

The Crusaders briefly managed to turn the tide when flanker Matt Todd went over in the 21st minute, but the rest of the match belonged to the tourists.

Brad Barritt became England's third try scorer when he dived over 12 minutes before the break, and there was still time for a fourth before the two teams regrouped in the dressing room when Slater stole the ball deep in enemy territory, and Goode made the most of his captain's pilfering to dummy his way over.

In truth, the opening moments of the second half became a little disjointed, as England made eight substitutions in the opening 20 minutes, but once the replacements had adjusted to the tempo of the match, the visitors rediscovered their rhythm.

The fifth try went to 20-year-old Bath wing Anthony Watson, a star of England Under-20s' 2013 IRB Junior World Championship triumph, after he sliced through the Crusaders' defence from 40 metres out and then outstripped the cover with a devastating burst of pace.

There was time for one more score, and it came in the 80th minute. Barritt opted for the grubber kick to turn the defence and Worcester full-back Chris Pennell, a 56th-minute replacement for Goode, was quickest to respond. Stephen Myler's conversion attempt went wide, but the final whistle sounded seconds later to confirm England as handsome winners.

"As a team I thought we had control of the game throughout and that's what's important," said Cipriani after the match. "The whole point was to make sure we put in a good performance everyone could be proud of. It was very important we gave the squad a lift going into the third Test."

Of course it was not a Test victory, but it was, nonetheless, a first success on New Zealand soil for an England senior side since 2003. The win underlined the genuine strength in depth in Lancaster's squad and although just two of the 23 who featured in Christchurch would be involved in the third

Test four days later (Cipriani and second row Dave Attwood were included on the bench), the performance of a young England XV was undoubtedly a cause for optimism for the future.

"The challenge was to put down a marker on Tuesday night to take that momentum into Saturday. What we didn't want was to face the All Blacks after not delivering to our full potential and everything is geared towards Saturday."

Stuart Lancaster

Crusaders 7		England 38	
15	Tom TAYLOR	15 →	Alex GOODE
14	Jimmy McNICHOLL	14	Ben FODEN
13 →	Reynold LEE-LO	13 →	Henry TRINDER
12 →	Kieron FONOTIA	12	Brad BARRITT
11	Nafi TUITAVAKE	11	Anthony WATSON
10	Tyler BLEYENDAAL	10 →	Danny CIPRIANI
9 →	Willi HEINZ	9 →	Lee DICKSON
1 →	Tim PERRY	1 →	Alex WALLER
2 →	Corey FLYNN	2 →	Joe GRAY
3 →	Nepo LUALALA	3 →	Henry THOMAS
4 →	Jimmy TUPOU	4	Ed SLATER
5	Joel EVERSON	5 →	Dave ATTWOOD
6	Jordan TAUFUA	6	James HASKELL
7 →	George WHITELOCK	7	Matt KVESIC
8	Luke WHITELOCK	8	Tom JOHNSON

REPLACEMENTS			REPLACEMENTS		
2 ←	16	Ben FUNNELL	2 ←	16	Dave WARD
1 ←	17	Joe MOODY	1 ←	17	Nathan CATT
3 ←	18	Siate TOKOLAHI	3 ←	18	Kyle SINCKLER
4 ←	19	Scott BARRETT	5 ←	19	Michael PATERSON
7 ←	20	Matt TODD	9 ←	20	Richard WIGGLESWORTH
9 ←	21	Andy ELLIS	10 ←	21	Stephen MYLER
12 ←	22	Adam WHITELOCK	13 ←	22	Jonny MAY
13 ←	23	Rob THOMPSON	15 ←	23	Chris PENNELL

SCORES

Try: Todd (21)

Con: Taylor (23)

SCORES

Tries: Gray (1), Foden (6), Barritt (28), Goode (33), Watson (58), Pennell (80)

Cons: Cipriani (2, 30, 35), Myler (59)

New Zealand vs England

THE THIRD TEST

With the series lost and both body and mind weary, England headed to Hamilton for the climax of the tour and a final roll of the dice. A mere six points had separated the Red Rose and the All Blacks in the first two titanic Tests, but the third clash in the Waikato Stadium was to prove a bridge too far for Stuart Lancaster's side.

England Rugby

NZL 36
ENG 13

Date: 21 June 2014
Stadium: Waikato
    Stadium, Hamilton
Attendance: 25,800
Referee: Jerome Garces
    (France)

Injuries on a tour that follows a prolonged and attritional domestic campaign are inevitable. Modern players may be incredible physical specimens, but rugby rarely takes any prisoners, and as Lancaster surveyed his options ahead of the third Test, the head coach found his resources had been depleted.

The first major casualty was fly-half Owen Farrell, who suffered remedial knee ligament damage and was ruled out. Second row Geoff Parling, a standout performer in the first two games, joined him on the treatment table with a hamstring injury.

It hardly constituted an injury crisis, but the enforced absentees, coupled with Lancaster's need to refresh the team, saw him make a total of seven changes to his starting XV, with Freddie Burns selected at 10, reforming the half-back partnership with Ben Youngs that featured in Auckland, while Courtney Lawes came in for Parling. Chris Ashton was handed his first Test start on the wing since November the previous year. Kyle Eastmond also came back into the team in midfield, while the big guns – in the shape of hooker Dylan Hartley and No.8 Billy

Left: Wing Julian Savea scored a hat-trick of tries for the All Blacks against England in the third Test in Hamilton.

Above: **No.8 Billy Vunipola was shown a yellow card in the 20th minutes of England's defeat in the Waikato Stadium.**

Vunipola – were restored to the pack.

New Zealand's prime motivation before kick-off was the opportunity to notch up a record-equalling 17th straight victory over a tier-one nation. While Lancaster insisted the match – and the tour as a whole – remained significant in terms of England's ongoing development.

"We don't see this third game as any sort of dead rubber whatsoever," he said in his pre-match press conference. "It's a hugely important game for us and for New Zealand. They want to build momentum heading into the Rugby Championship, and we want to finish the season strongly.

"The ability to learn who can and who can't deliver at the highest level has been absolutely invaluable [on this tour]. You can watch as many DVDs and games as you like, but it's only when you get your hands on players week in week out that you really learn the true strengths of individuals."

It turned out to be the proverbial game of two halves in Hamilton: and the first was a nightmare for the tourists, as New Zealand ran riot, scoring four unanswered tries that essentially ended the game as contest.

The floodgates opened as early as the third minute, when Ben Smith's pass put Julian Savea away on the left wing and full-back Mike Brown could not get across in time to avert the danger. Burns knocked over a penalty shortly afterwards, after Aaron Smith had been caught offside at a ruck, but Savea helped himself to a second try just a minute later after Aaron Cruden's long pass split England's defence.

A second successful Burns penalty briefly kept the tourists in the hunt, but disaster struck when Vunipola was sin binned for a high tackle on Cruden. While the Saracens man was contemplating the error of his ways in the dugout, New Zealand went over again when Aaron Smith took a precision pass from Cory Jane on the right wing.

England were on the ropes and the All Blacks went for the jugular, extending their lead to 29–6 by half time, with a second Aaron Smith try seven minutes before the break.

By the players' own admission after

the match, there was some serious soul-searching in the dressing room at half time. The collective performance had not been acceptable and it was a rejuvenated and far more ferocious England XV that emerged in the second half.

The tourists' renewed commitment was quickly rewarded with a try. Launchbury made the initial break in midfield, and as he was dragged down, he found Youngs in close support. The Leicester scrum-half scampered into the Kiwi 22 and passed to Manu Tuilagi, who tried to power his way over the line. It took three All Blacks to stop him inches short, but England recycled the ball quickly and Marland Yarde was on hand to pick up and drive over from close range. Burns landed the conversion and although New Zealand were still 29–13 in front, England had finally made a statement.

They came agonizingly close to a second try moments later. It was Yarde again who asked the question, hammering his way over the line from five metres out, but the combined attentions of Richie McCaw, Aaron Smith and Jane prevented the wing from grounding the ball and there was no score.

England continued to pose the greater attacking threat as the half unfolded, and another eye-catching break from Yarde in the opposition 22 set off alarm bells in the New Zealand ranks. But as hard as the Red Rose pressed, they could not find their way through the home side's abrasive defence.

The match had entered second-half injury time when Savea completed his hat-trick. It was a cruel end to the match after England had gone so far to redeeming themselves in the second period, but the final scoreline of 36–13 to the All Blacks made for sobering reading.

England could at least draw some comfort from the knowledge that they had held the world champions 7–7 in the second half. It was a creditable recovery after their first-half woes, which highlighted the strength of character in the squad. After the final whistle, Ben Youngs acknowledged that the half-time dressing-room dissection of the team's failings had been central to the turnaround.

"They were honest words, this is an honest group," he said. "We pride ourselves on defence and spend a lot of time on it, but the first half wasn't good enough. Whether it was individual mistakes or collectively we'll have

to have a look, but you can't give them that big a lead and expect to be in the game

"We let ourselves down and left ourselves with a mountain to climb. Against New Zealand you can't leave yourself with such a huge chase and we paid the price. The second half things came off a little bit more, but the damage was done. We put in great performances before this, but you'll remember how we did in the last game. Unfortunately, today puts a dampener on what we did in the first games.

"It's just tough lessons against these boys. This is a young squad with a World Cup coming up, and it's about getting more and more experience. Unfortunately, you have to go through these games to get experience."

England's tour was over. A rare Test victory on New Zealand soil had not been forthcoming, but as the players dispersed for their hard-earned holidays, Lancaster could reflect on a trip on which the positives far outweighed the negatives.

"We've learnt a lot about the players, without any doubt," he said. "We'll take that into next season and we'll build. We have a World Cup squad to pick in a year's time and we need to get everything right."

Above: **Freddie Burns is grabbed around the waist by Ma'a Nonu during the third Test at Waikato Stadium.**

Right: **Wing Marland Yarde was England's solitary try-scorer in the 36–13 defeat in the third Test at Hamilton.**

"Against the All Blacks, you need to be proactive in what you do, not reactive, and the minute you're behind the gainline it becomes a snowball and we didn't stop it for 25 minutes."

Andy Farrell

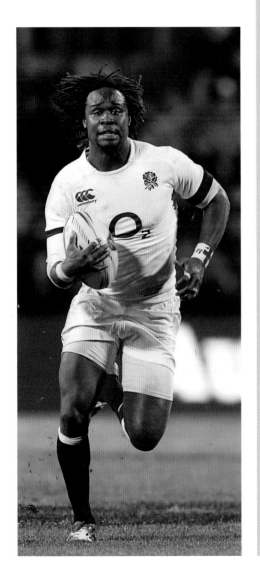

New Zealand 36	England 13
15 Ben **Smith**	15 Mike **BROWN**
14 Cory **JANE**	14 Chris **ASHTON**
13 → Malakai **FEKITOA**	13 Manusamoa **TUILAGI**
12 Ma'a **NONU**	12 → Kyle **EASTMOND**
11 Julian **SAVEA**	11 Marland **YARDE**
10 → Aaron **CRUDEN**	10 → Freddie **BURNS**
9 → Aaron **SMITH**	9 → Ben **YOUNGS**
1 → Tony **WOODCOCK**	1 → Joe **MARLER**
2 → Dane **COLES**	2 → Dylan **HARTLEY**
3 → Owen **FRANKS**	3 → David **WILSON**
4 → Brodie **RETALLICK**	4 → Joe **LAUNCHBURY**
5 Sam **WHITELOCK**	5 Courtney **LAWES**
6 → Jerome **KAINO**	6 Tom **WOOD**
7 Richie **McCAW** (c)	7 Chris **ROBSHAW** (c)
8 → Kieran **READ**	8 → Billy **VUNIPOLA**

REPLACEMENTS	REPLACEMENTS
2 ← 16 Keven **MEALAMU**	2 ← 16 Rob **WEBBER**
1 ← 17 Wyatt **CROCKETT**	1 ← 17 Matt **MULLAN**
3 ← 18 Charlie **FAUMUINA**	3 ← 18 Kieran **BROOKES**
4 ← 19 Patrick **TUIPULOTU**	4 ← 19 Dave **ATTWOOD**
8 ← 20 Liam **MESSAM**	8 ← 20 Ben **MORGAN**
9 ← 21 TJ **PERENARA**	9 ← 21 Lee **DICKSON**
10 ← 22 Beauden **BARRETT**	10 ← 22 Danny **CIPRIANI**
13 ← 23 Ryan **CROTTY**	12 ← 23 Luther **BURRELL**

SCORES

Tries: Savea (3, 8, 80), AL Smith (26, 33)

Cons: Cruden (9, 27, 34), Barrett (82)

Pen: Cruden (17)

SCORES

Try: Yarde (42)

Con: Burns (43)

Pens: Burns (7, 19)

New Zealand		England
28	Kicks from hand	28
163	Passes	124
133	Runs	92
617	Metres run with ball	387
53%	Possession	47%
58%	Territory	42%
14	Clean breaks	7
30	Defenders beaten	14
14	Offloads	15
76 from 83	Rucks won	62 from 65
6 from 6	Mauls won	8 from 9
16	Turnovers conceded	23
100/14	Tackles (made/missed)	132/30
88.0%	Tackling success rate	81.0%
7 won, 0 lost (100.0%)	Scrums on own feed	8 won, 2 lost (80.0%)
15 won, 4 lost (78.9%)	Lineouts on own throw	16 won, 2 lost (88.9%)
14 (2)	Penalties conceded (freekicks)	8 (0)
1/0	Yellow/red cards	1/0

IN PROFILE:

Luther Burrell

Test rugby is rarely an environment that offers second chances. The onus on those thrust into the international arena is to make an immediate impact, and Burrell did just that when he was drafted into the England side ahead of the 2014 RBS 6 Nations.

England
Rugby

Position: **Centre**
Age: **27**
Height: **1.91m**
Weight: **109kg**
Caps: **7**

It was a mixture of good form and good fortune that saw Luther Burrell handed his England debut for the championship opener against France in Paris. His explosive performances for Northampton undoubtedly spoke for themselves, but the Saints star was also indebted to Lady Luck for his breakthrough.

The door was left ajar after Manu Tuilagi failed to shake off a chest injury. It swung dramatically open when Joel Tomkins, who had started in all three of the autumn internationals the previous year, was sidelined with a knee problem, and as Stuart Lancaster surveyed his selection options, Burrell was the next cab off the rank.

His glorious dash to the line on debut for England's second try against France was a special moment. His irresistible burst through the Scottish midfield at Murrayfield seven days later set the platform for the Red Rose's comprehensive victory, and when he outpaced the Welsh cover at Twickenham for his third try in just four appearances, there was no doubt that England had unearthed a finisher of the highest order.

With the World Cup looming, Burrell's arrival was as spectacular as it was timely, and was all the more impressive given that he was deployed at outside centre by England rather than in the 12 berth that he had made his own at Franklin's Gardens.

His elevation to the side renewed a relationship with Lancaster that dated back to when the England coach was in charge of the Academy at Leeds Carnegie between 2001 and 2006. Back then, Burrell was a teenager making his way in the game, having turned his back on rugby league and a junior career with the Huddersfield Giants.

Buoyed by his success with England, Burrell was also in superlative form for Northampton in 2014, playing a pivotal part in the club's domestic and European double after victories over Bath in the Challenge Cup final and Saracens in the Premiership final at Twickenham.

> "Luther is an inspiration to any young player. He has worked extremely hard to get to where he is now and others would do well to follow that example."

Alex King, Northampton Saints coach

His inclusion in Lancaster's squad for the tour of New Zealand in the summer was little more than a formality and, although no Saints players were considered for selection for the first match in Auckland because of fixture congestion, he featured against the All Blacks in both the second and third Tests.

As typifies many former league players, Burrell embodies pace, power and defensive solidity in perfect harmony, while 13 Premiership tries in his first two seasons with Northampton since signing from Sale in 2012 testify to his eye for the line. His England career is still in its infancy, but no one could accuse the centre of not making the most of the opportunities that have so far come his way.

Opposite: **Luther Burrell scored his first international try on his debut, against France in Paris in the 2014 RBS 6 Nations Championship.**

Chris Robshaw holds aloft the Cook Cup following England's victory over Australia in the last of the autumn internationals.

The QBE Internationals

The annual autumn Tests saw England entertain New Zealand, South Africa, Samoa and Australia at Twickenham on consecutive Saturdays in November, and afforded Stuart Lancaster's side a valuable opportunity to assess their strength against southern hemisphere opposition one final time before the start of the World Cup in 2015.

The four matches were to prove an unrelenting examination of the Red Rose's resources as Lancaster negotiated a debilitating injury list, but his team emerged from the series with its pride intact and many individual reputations, particularly among the more recent additions to the squad, were enhanced.

Narrow, three-point defeats to the All Blacks and the Springboks in the opening two Tests were undeniably bitter pills to swallow, but England's collective character and power came to the fore as they recovered from those setbacks to record victories over the Samoans and the Wallabies.

England saved their best performance of the series for the closing weekend and their triumph over Australia, a fixture that will be repeated when the two countries meet at HQ in the group stages of the World Cup in October, but there was also much to admire in the way the Red Rose battled with vastly more experienced New Zealand and South Africa sides.

England remain a work in progress, but on the evidence of the QBE Internationals, the team is tantalizingly close to completing their journey.

England vs New Zealand

A CLOSE CONTEST

England
Rugby

ENG 21
NZL 24

Date: 8 November 2014
Stadium: **Twickenham**
Attendance: **82,223**
Referee: **Nigel Owens**
(Wales)

The All Blacks arrived at Twickenham in November fresh from the successful defence of their Rugby Championship crown, while England were in the midst of a crippling injury crisis. The odds were stacked heavily against Stuart Lancaster's men, but they responded heroically to push the reigning world champions to the limit.

Familiarity breeds contempt according to the old adage, but as England and New Zealand prepared to cross swords for a fifth time in the space of a year, the level of anticipation at HQ was undiminished. The All Blacks' 22nd visit to Twickenham since the first Test between the two sides at the ground in 1925 was nothing if not box office, and HQ was once again bursting at the seams.

It was the Red Rose's first international since they had faced the Kiwis in Hamilton five months earlier, but as Lancaster prepared his troops for the fray, he could have been forgiven for feeling a certain sense of injustice as he surveyed his depleted squad deprived of no less than eight potential starters through injury.

It was a body blow ahead of such an important fixture, and the withdrawals prompted Lancaster to hand an international debut to Bath wing Semesa Rokoduguni, while the uncapped duo of Saracens second row George Kruis and 20-year-old Bath flyer Anthony Watson were named on the bench.

If England were apprehensive before kick-off it did not show and Lancaster's team made a sensational start with a breathtaking third-minute try. The pack secured possession, the ball went through the hands of Danny Care, Owen Farrell and then the recalled Brad Barritt and, with England on the halfway line, the next pass found Gloucester wing Jonny May.

The New Zealand defence appeared well marshalled, but May was unperturbed and his initial burst of pace took him effortlessly past Conrad Smith and over the gain line. The Kiwis desperately tried to get back, but May was now in full flight and his momentum

Below left: **All Black captain Richie McCaw scored his side's second try at Twickenham.**

Below: **England came agonisingly close to toppling the reigning world champions at HQ.**

and a delicate step took him outside full-back Israel Dagg and over the line for a superb solo try – his first in his eighth Test appearance.

England were utterly dominant at this stage, but they were ultimately to pay a heavy price for their failure to turn their initial superiority into points. Three penalties from Farrell before the break kept the scoreboard ticking over, but the All Blacks got a foothold in the game with an Aaron Cruden try and two successful penalties from the Kiwi fly-half.

England led 14–11 at half time, but when they failed to replicate the same level of intensity they had showed in the first 40 minutes after the restart, the tourists began to take control. A try from captain Richie McCaw five minutes into the half put New Zealand in front for the first time in the match and they stretched their advantage to 24–14 in the 71st minute when substitute prop Charlie Faumuina barged his way over after the All Blacks had gone through what proved to be an irresistible 20 phases of play.

Lancaster's team were now desperate for points, but they were to come too late to mount what would have been a famous fightback. An attacking scrum just metres from the try line saw the England front row outmuscle their Kiwi counterparts, and as the tourists' scrum disintegrated under the weight of the drive, referee Nigel Owens had no hesitation in awarding a penalty try. Replacement fly-half George Ford hastily added a dropped conversion in front of the posts, but there were just seconds remaining on the clock and the All Blacks were able to hold out for a 24–21 victory.

For the third time in their last four meetings with the World Cup holders, England had been beaten by five points or less and, although defeat was a bitter pill to swallow, Lancaster was adamant the performance at Twickenham was further evidence of his young side's improvement.

"We haven't got the right result, but we don't feel we're far away," he said. "In the first half we were pretty close, if not level. We've had one-and-a-half week's preparation and we've got young lads who are 20 and 21 years old making their debuts at Twickenham against the All Blacks. The performance of the pack was excellent. We put a lot of pressure on their ball and there was some good rugby on show in the first half."

England 21		New Zealand 24	
15	Mike BROWN	15	Israel DAGG
14 →	Semesa ROKODUGUNI	14	Ben SMITH
13	Brad BARRITT	13 →	Conrad SMITH
12 →	Kyle EASTMOND	12	Sonny Bill WILLIAMS
11	Jonny MAY	11	Julian SAVEA
10	Owen FARRELL	10 →	Aaron CRUDEN
9 →	Danny CARE	9 →	Aaron SMITH
1 →	Joe MARLER	1 →	Wyatt CROCKETT
2 →	Dylan HARTLEY	2 →	Dane COLES
3 →	David WILSON	3 →	Owen FRANKS
4	Dave ATTWOOD	4	Brodie RETALLICK
5 →	Courtney LAWES	5	Sam WHITELOCK
6	Tom WOOD	6 →	Jerome KAINO
7	Chris ROBSHAW (c)	7	Richie MCCAW (c)
8 →	Billy VUNIPOLA	8	Kieran READ

REPLACEMENTS			REPLACEMENTS		
2 ←	16 Rob WEBBER		2 ←	16 Keven MEALAMU	
1 ←	17 Matt MULLAN		1 ←	17 Ben FRANKS	
3 ←	18 Kieran BROOKES		3 ←	18 Charlie FAUMUINA	
5 ←	19 George KRUIS		4 ←	19 Patrick TUIPULOTU	
8 ←	20 Ben MORGAN		16 ←	20 Liam MESSAM	
9 ←	21 Ben YOUNGS		9 ←	21 TJ PERENARA	
12 ←	22 George FORD		10 ←	22 Beauden BARRETT	
14 ←	23 Anthony WATSON		1 ←	23 Ryan CROTTY	

SCORES	SCORES
Tries: May (3), Penalty try (79)	Tries: Cruden (13), McCaw (45), Faumuina (71)
Cons: Ford (79)	Cons:
Pens: Farrell (17, 21, 40)	Pens: Cruden (23, 36), Barrett (65)

"I feel as though that has been coming for a while now. It's almost a demon off the back to get that first try. I knew I could do it and the coaches knew I could as well. I'm glad they've shown patience in me and that I've been able to pay them back. Hopefully it's the first of many tries and I can move forward from here."

Jonny May

England vs South Africa

THREE POINTS SHORT

ENG 28
RSA 31

Date: **15 November 2014**
Stadium: **Twickenham**
Attendance: **82,125**
Referee: **Steve Walsh** (New Zealand)

The second QBE International of the series brought the Springboks to London and presented England with another opportunity to claim a coveted southern hemisphere scalp. South Africa had come away from Twickenham a year earlier with a narrow 16–15 victory, but 12 months on the Red Rose were determined to avenge that result against the two-time world champions.

When Stuart Lancaster took up the reins as England head coach, he was acutely aware that victories over South Africa, Australia and New Zealand had become a frustrating rarity. The Red Rose's record against the southern hemisphere "big three" was in urgent need of improvement.

Within a year of his appointment, Lancaster's side had famously beaten the All Blacks at Twickenham. In 2013, they despatched the Wallabies at HQ, but despite a 14–14 draw with the Springboks in Port Elizabeth in the third Test in the summer of 2012, a triumph over Heyneke Meyer's side had eluded England.

The clash with South Africa at Twickenham in November was the fifth meeting between the two sides since Lancaster's promotion, and he made just one change to the starting XV that had faced the All Blacks seven days earlier, handing a first Test start to wing Anthony Watson in place of his injured Bath team-mate Semesa Rokoduguni.

The South Africa side included five players who had featured in the 2007 World Cup final victory over England, and with a combined total of 1,011 caps in Meyer's match-day squad (compared England's modest 467), the contrast in experience could not have been starker.

In a match that yielded six tries, there was just one in the first half at HQ – a Jan Serfontein interception from a Danny Care pass – and as the two sides headed to the dressing room at the break, the Springboks had established a 13–6 lead. However, the first 40 minutes were merely the calm before

the storm, and the Twickenham faithful were to witness a pulsating second period in which England nearly edged to victory.

South Africa struck first with an early score from scrum-half Cobus Reinach, but just as it appeared the visitors might pull clear, England came roaring back with a two-try salvo that dramatically changed the complexion of the game.

The first score came in the 44th minute as the pack caught and drove from an attacking lineout. The rolling maul that followed was irresistible and it was Bath prop David Wilson who supplied the all-important touchdown as the forwards swept aside their Springbok counterparts. England unleashed another devastating maul three minutes later from which substitute No. 8 Ben Morgan sprang, powering his way past, and then through, five South African players for the try. Owen Farrell added the routine conversion, as he had for Wilson's score, and the match was suddenly all square at 20–20.

The Springboks were on the ropes, but they

Above: **Jan Serfontein opens the scoring for the Springboks with an interception try.**

Opposite: **England celebrate after Ben Morgan powered his way over for a second try for the Red Rose.**

> "We are probably not doing ourselves justice. We all know the way we train and the way we want to play and we haven't put it on the pitch as well as we would have liked."

Chris Robshaw

England 28		South Africa 31	
15	Mike BROWN	15	Willie LE ROUX
14	Anthony WATSON	14	JP PIETERSEN
13	Brad BARRITT	13	Jan SERFONTEIN
12	Kyle EASTMOND	12	Jean DE VILLIERS (c)
11	Jonny MAY	11	Bryan HABANA
10 →	Owen FARRELL	10	Pat LAMBIE
9 →	Danny CARE	9	Cobus REINACH
1 →	Joe MARLER	1 →	Tendai MTAWARIRA
2 →	Dylan HARTLEY	2 →	Adriaan STRAUSS
3 →	David WILSON	3 →	Jannie DU PLESSIS
4 →	Dave ATTWOOD	4 →	Eben ETZEBETH
5	Courtney LAWES	5	Victor MATFIELD
6	Tom WOOD	6	Marcell COETZEE
7	Chris ROBSHAW (c)	7 →	Schalk BURGER
8 →	Billy VUNIPOLA	8	Duane VERMEULEN

REPLACEMENTS		REPLACEMENTS	
2 ←	16 Rob WEBBER	2 ←	16 Bismarck DU PLESSIS
1 ←	17 Matt MULLAN	1 ←	17 Trevor NYAKANE
3 ←	18 Kieran BROOKES	3 ←	18 Coenie OOSTHUIZEN
4 ←	19 George KRUIS	4 ←	19 Bakkies BOTHA
8 ←	20 Ben MORGAN	7 ←	20 Oupa MOHOJE
9 ←	21 Ben YOUNGS		21 Francois HOUGAARD
10 ←	22 George FORD		22 Handre POLLARD
	23 Marland YARDE		23 Cornal HENDRICKS

SCORES

Tries: **Wilson (44), Morgan (47), Barritt (78)**

Cons: **Farrell (45, 48)**

Pens: **Farrell (27, 35), Ford (67)**

SCORES

Tries: **Serfontein (15), Reinach (40), Burger (53)**

Cons: **Lambie (15, 41)**

Pens: **Lambie (10, 32, 66)**

Drops: **Lambie (76)**

fell back on their collective experience to regain a foothold in the contest. Flanker Schalk Burger barged his way over for their third try in the 53rd minute, despite veteran second row Victor Matfield being sent to the sin bin, while fly-half Pat Lambie knocked over a penalty and a drop goal to put the visitors eight points in front.

England were not finished though, and when Saracens centre Brad Barritt squeezed over in the corner with just two minutes remaining, there was renewed hope. The attempted conversion from George Ford went wide, however, and although England were just three points adrift, the clock denied them the chance to complete a glorious fightback. For a second successive weekend, Lancaster's side had left it too late to turn the tide and had again been beaten by a southern hemisphere side by a single score.

"It's not the end of the world," insisted flanker Tom Wood after the final whistle. "It's disappointing to lose in an England shirt and you never want to accept that, particularly at home. But the fact we have lost by two really close margins in two really competitive games against the two best teams in the world doesn't mean it's back to the drawing board.

"We have to keep our heads high and keep believing in what we are trying to implement. We understand we will come under a lot of pressure now. The heat is going to come on from the rugby media and the rugby public. All we can do is stay tight as a group and keep plugging away."

England v Samoa

BACK TO WINNING WAYS

With six victories from their previous six meetings against the powerful Pacific Islanders since the maiden clash between the two countries in 1995, Stuart Lancaster's charges prepared for the penultimate QBE International of the series against Samoa confident they could rediscover their winning touch and end their five-Test losing streak.

England Rugby

ENG 28
SAM 9

Date: **22 November 2014**
Stadium: **Twickenham**
Attendance: **82,076**
Referee: **Jaco Peyper (South Africa)**

The squad regrouped to tackle the Samoans at HQ, with the players remaining resolutely upbeat. The Red Rose had taken the collective decision to focus on the future rather than dwelling on the "what ifs" of the past fortnight.

The sense of moving forward was reflected in Lancaster's bold selection for the match. The coach made five changes, and he signalled his intent to continue England's evolution with the headline-grabbing inclusion of 21-year-old Bath fly-half George Ford. All of Ford's four previous caps had been from the bench, but Lancaster decided the time had come for the youngster, the

Player of the Tournament at the IRB Junior World Championship in 2011, to graduate to the starting XV.

The move necessitated Owen Farrell's switch to inside centre for the first time since Italy in Rome in 2012, while Ben Youngs was recalled at scrum-half at the expense of Danny Care. In the pack, Rob Webber was named at hooker, No. 8 Ben Morgan replaced Billy Vunipola, while James Haskell took over blindside duties from Tom Wood.

It was, in truth, a frustrating first quarter at Twickenham, with a Tusi Pisi penalty for the visitors the only incident to trouble the scoreboard, but HQ was rewarded for

Below left: Full-back Mike Brown scores his sixth try against the Samoans at Twickenham.

Below: Fly-half George Ford marked his first start for England with 13 points.

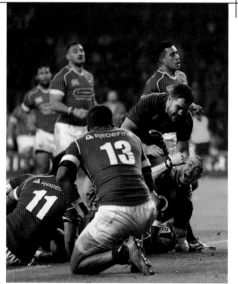

its patience midway through the half when England burst into life and scored a beautiful try through Jonny May. Courtney Lawes secured lineout possession; the ball went wide; Ford looped behind Farrell; and he found Mike Brown, who in turn passed inside to May. The Gloucester wing was still five metres shy of the Samoa 22, but an electric burst of pace from a standing start took him past the initial line of defence and the Gloucester flier had sufficient momentum to get over the line. Ford converted effortlessly and England were in business.

Two penalties from Ford either side of the break extended the advantage, but it was England's two second-half tries that were to seal their victory and cheer the Twickenham faithful. The first came in the 45th minute and owed much to the vision and precision of Ford as the fly-half produced a sumptuous cross-field kick that Anthony Watson gathered, and although the right wing was hauled down just short of what would have been his first Test try, he had the awareness to offload to Brown, who had the simple task of touching down. Ford added the conversion.

Seven minutes later, the Red Rose had their third try. The first two had been the exclusive work of the backs, but this time it was the pack who were the creators, as quick hands in midfield from Chris Robshaw, Dave Attwood and then Joe Marler opened up the space out wide and May merely had to scamper over from five metres out.

England were unable to fashion any further tries at Twickenham, but after the agonies of the previous two weekends, their final 28–9 victory was a significant morale boost and evidence that the team had been bruised but unbowed by their opening two autumn international defeats.

"It was a tough, physical Samoa side to play against, but George Ford's performance was a step in the right direction for him," Lancaster said at full time. "He's so young as a player in international terms, but he's someone who's going to be around a long time for England. It was a great first start for him. He looked calm, he looked composed and he controlled the game well. He was incisive at line breaks. This means Owen's now got some genuine competition at 10, but also we've got the option of looking at Owen at 12.

"We've got a very good young team developing who have never been smashed or taken apart by any team we've come up against. While we improved against Samoa, I still feel there's another 10–15 per cent to go to beat Australia next week."

> "Samoa are always going to be a little bit different because they are massive men who love the physical battle. I wouldn't say it was enjoyable to take those hits, but you've got to do it."
>
> **George Ford**

England 28		Samoa 9	
15	Mike BROWN	15	Ken PISI
14	Anthony WATSON	14	Alapati LEIUA
13	Brad BARRITT	13	Rey LEE-LO
12 →	Owen FARRELL	12	Johnny LEOTA
11 →	Jonny MAY	11	David LEMI (c)
10	George FORD	10 →	Tusi PISI
9 →	Ben YOUNGS	9	Kahn FOTUALI'I
1 →	Joe MARLER	1 →	Zak TAULAFO
2	Rob WEBBER	2 →	Ti'i PAULO
3	David WILSON	3 →	Census JOHNSTON
4	Dave ATTWOOD	4 →	Filo PAULO
5 →	Courtney LAWES	5 →	Kane THOMPSON
6 →	James HASKELL	6	Maurie FA'ASAVALU
7	Chris ROBSHAW (c)	7 →	Jack LAM
8	Ben MORGAN	8	Ofisa TREVIRANUS

REPLACEMENTS		REPLACEMENTS	
2 ←	16 Dylan HARTLEY	2 ←	16 Manu LEIATAUA
1 ←	17 Matt MULLAN	1 ←	17 Viliamu AFATIA
3 ←	18 Kieran BROOKES	3 ←	18 Anthony PERENISE
5 ←	19 George KRUIS	4 ←	19 Fa'atiga LEMALU
6 ←	20 Tom WOOD	5 ←	20 Dan LEO
9 ←	21 Richard WIGGLESWORTH	7 ←	21 TJ IOANE
12 ←	22 Billy TWELVETREES		22 Pele COWLEY
11 ←	23 Marland YARDE	10 ←	23 Mike STANLEY

SCORES

Tries: **May** (19, 52), **Brown** (45)

Cons: **Ford** (20, 46)

Pens: **Ford** (17, 26, 41)

SCORES

Pens: **T Pisi** (3, 23, 49)

England vs Australia

SAVING THE BEST TILL LAST

The climax of the QBE Internationals presented the Red Rose with a third and final chance to defeat SANZAR opposition at HQ and to finish the year with a significant flourish. England craved a victory over the Wallabies and, thanks to a Herculean effort from the pack, they were to emerge triumphant at Twickenham.

England Rugby

ENG 26
AUS 17

Date: **29 November 2014**
Stadium: **Twickenham**
Attendance: **82,049**
Referee: **Jerome Garces** (France)

An Anglo-Australian Test match needs no hyperbolic build-up to whet the appetite. Any meeting between the two countries is one to savour, but with the two teams scheduled to meet in the group stages of the 2015 World Cup, the sense of anticipation ahead of what was essentially a dress rehearsal for their pivotal Pool A encounter was only heightened.

The Wallabies would present a sterner challenge than Samoa had the previous weekend, but nonetheless the head coach kept faith in the majority of the personnel who had toppled the Pacific Islanders.

The return of hooker Dylan Hartley and flanker Tom Wood to the fray, in place of Rob Webber and James Haskell respectively, was widely predicted, but Lancaster did have one surprising selection to unveil, recalling Gloucester's Billy Twelvetrees at inside centre at the expense of Owen Farrell.

The match was Australia's 23rd visit to Twickenham and the visitors were quickest out of the blocks, taking a third-minute lead through a Bernard Foley penalty. England replied with two penalties from Bath fly-half George Ford to edge into a lead they would not surrender for the rest of the match.

The first try of the afternoon went to the Red Rose after 28 minutes, and was built on the growing dominance of the England forwards. A scrum in the Wallaby 22 saw the home side march the Australians backwards, and when the ball was moved wide, Brad Barritt made the hard yards in midfield. Possession was quickly recycled and after an incisive interchange between Ben Youngs

and Wood, No. 8 Ben Morgan took the pass and muscled his way over the line, despite the attentions of three tacklers.

The Wallabies hit back early in the second half with a well-worked score from Foley, but England were in no mood to relinquish their advantage, and they capitalized on their set-piece superiority once again in the 56th minute with another try from Morgan. England had the put-in at a scrum five metres short of the Australian line, Hartley successfully hooked and with the ball at the base, the home side turned on the power and the Wallaby front five rapidly disintegrated. Morgan deftly picked up and rumbled his way through the ruins of the Wallaby scrum for his second try of the match.

Ford's second successful conversion made

Above: **Ben Morgan was England's hero with two tries against the Wallabies.**

> "We always believed in the plan and believed in the players this week. There was a real single-minded approach to the game we wanted to take. I thought we took it and the players applied the plan really well."

Stuart Lancaster

it 20–10 to Lancaster's side, but if England were in danger of becoming complacent, they were quickly reminded the job was far from finished when substitute flanker Will Skelton forced his way over two minutes later. Quade Cooper knocked over the conversion and the Wallabies were suddenly only 20–17 adrift.

It was time for cool heads to close the match out, and that responsibility fell to 21-year-old Ford, who belied his international inexperience with nerveless penalties in the 63rd and 76th minutes to deflate the Wallaby fightback and seal a morale-boosting 26–17 victory.

With a second successive win over Australia at HQ, England had retained the Cook Cup but, more significantly, the Red Rose had claimed a southern hemisphere scalp and laid down a muscular marker ahead of their World Cup campaign.

"We played intelligently and the boys executed the game plan," Lancaster said after the final whistle. "The scrum and maul were excellent. You have to play rugby in different ways. Against New Zealand and South Africa, our game management let us down. Today our game management was much better.

"The best thing to restore belief is winning. We had very frank discussions after New Zealand and South Africa, but you always need to look forward. We've got a great young set of lads and today it was all about getting a win against a big nation.

"We have not got everything right by any stretch of the imagination. There's still a lot of work to do, but I think the leadership shown by

George [Ford] and Ben Youngs in particular was excellent. One of the most pleasing things overall, if you look back at 2014, irrespective of today's result, was that we scored 26 tries, and 21 of those were by the backs."

England 26		Australia 17	
15	Mike BROWN	15	Israel FOLAU
14	Anthony WATSON	14 →	Henry SPEIGHT
13 →	Brad BARRITT	13	Adam ASHLEY-COOPER
12 →	Billy TWELVETREES	12	Matt TOOMUA
11	Jonny MAY	11	Rob HORNE
10	George FORD	10 →	Bernard FOLEY
9 →	Ben YOUNGS	9 →	Nick PHIPPS
1 →	Joe MARLER	1 →	James SLIPPER
2 →	Dylan HARTLEY	2 →	Saia FAINGA'A
3 →	David WILSON	3 →	Sekope KEPU
4	Dave ATTWOOD	4	Sam CARTER
5 →	Courtney LAWES	5 →	Rob SIMMONS
6	Tom WOOD	6 →	Sean MCMAHON
7	Chris ROBSHAW (c)	7	Michael HOOPER (c)
8	Ben MORGAN	8	Ben MCCALMAN

REPLACEMENTS		REPLACEMENTS	
2 ←	16 Rob WEBBER	2 ←	16 James HANSON
1 ←	17 Matt MULLAN	1 ←	17 Benn ROBINSON
3 ←	18 Kieran BROOKES	3 ←	18 Ben ALEXANDER
	19 George KRUIS	6 ←	19 Will SKELTON
5 ←	20 James HASKELL	5 ←	20 Luke JONES
9 ←	21 Richard WIGGLESWORTH	9 ←	21 Nic WHITE
13 ←	22 Owen FARRELL	10 ←	22 Quade COOPER
12 ←	23 Marland YARDE	14 ←	23 Kurtley BEALE

SCORES	SCORES
Tries: **Morgan (28, 56)**	Tries: **Foley (44), Skelton (59)**
Cons: **Ford (29, 57)**	Cons: **Foley (45), Cooper (60)**
Pens: **Ford (6, 12, 63, 76)**	Pens: **Foley (3)**

Below: England celebrate retaining the Cook Cup after their 26-17 victory over Australia.

IN PROFILE:

Joe Launchbury

In the old days, second-row forwards were gnarled and nasty specimens who powered the engine room and who were as likely to haul down a winger in full flight on the touchline as they were to put on some moisturizer before a match. Times change, however, and in Joe Launchbury, England boast the epitome of modern rugby's new breed of all-action locks.

England Rugby

Position: **Lock**
Age: **23**
Height: **1.98m**
Weight: **117kg**
Caps: **22**

Danny Care's try and eight points from the boot of Owen Farrell may have provided the platform for England's tense 13–10 victory over Ireland at Twickenham in the 2014 RBS 6 Nations Championship, but it was Joe Launchbury's dramatic tap tackle on wing Dave Kearney in the dying seconds of the match that ultimately ensured the Red Rose emerged victorious at HQ.

Exactly how the Wasps forward got anywhere near the Leinster flyer after 80 minutes of gruelling trench war with the Irish pack, let alone made contact with him, might be a mystery to second rows of a former vintage, but for those who have witnessed Launchbury's rapid development in Test rugby, his intervention came as little surprise.

First capped from the bench against Fiji in November 2012 at the age of 21, the lock made such an initial impact on proceedings that he earned a place in Stuart Lancaster's starting XV for the famous victory over the All Blacks the following month. At the end of the autumn, and after just four Test appearances, he was named the England Player of the Series. A star was born.

Not bad for a player who was released by the Harlequins Academy as a teenager and forced to drop down to National League 2 South level with Worthing in search of regular first-team rugby before returning to the upper echelons of the game when Wasps picked him up in 2010.

Despite his relative inexperience,

Launchbury has gone from strength to strength since making his international bow, and it spoke volumes that his omission from Warren Gatland's squad for the British and Irish Lions tour of Australia in the summer of 2013 was greeted by many with genuine dismay.

His athleticism and speed invariably catch

> "Being an international second row, you can't get pushed aside. You have to be right at the front."

Joe Launchbury

the eye, but the Wasps man never shirks the more traditional duties demanded of a second row, either in the lineout or at the breakdown, and he plays with a muscular belligerence that belies his lack of years. Launchbury may be supremely comfortable with the ball in hand out wide, but he is also the proverbial immovable object around the fringes.

Still only 23, he now has two full 6 Nations campaigns, a brutal but character-building tour of Argentina and the recent three-Test series against the All Blacks in New Zealand under his belt. He has already played in sides that have toppled the All Blacks and the Wallabies and, although he has had to grow up fast on the Test stage against older and wiser opponents, the new boy is fast becoming one of England's older heads.

Right: Lock Joe Launchbury enjoyed an outstanding RBS 6 Nations Championship campaign in 2014 as England clinched the Triple Crown.

IN PROFILE:

The England Coaching Staff

Behind every great Test team there's invariably an outstanding coaching staff, and England are fortunate to boast four of the most astute and respected men in the business.

STUART LANCASTER —
HEAD COACH

The Cumbrian played his club rugby for Leeds at flanker and represented Scotland at Under-21 level, but it as a coach that Lancaster has made his name, succeeding Martin Johnson as head coach ahead of the 2012 RBS 6 Nations campaign.

Lancaster retired as a player in 2000 and the following year was appointed the head of the Carnegie's Academy before becoming the club's director of rugby in 2005, steering Leeds back into the Premiership two years later after claiming the National Division One title.

His long-standing association with the RFU began in 2007, when he was unveiled as the head of Elite Player Development. It was a role that saw Lancaster take overall responsibility of all the age group and development sides, and during his tenure the England Saxons won the Churchill Cup three times while the England Under-20 team reached four out of five IRB Junior World Championship finals.

Such success made him a natural choice to replace Johnson after the 2011 World Cup. He was initially given the job on an interim basis, but after his team finished second in the 2012 RBS 6 Nations, he was offered a permanent, four-year contract. That deal was extended in October 2014, and he is now under contract with the RFU until 2020.

Since becoming head coach, England have beaten every other tier-one nation with the exception of South Africa, while the highlight of his reign came in the autumn of 2012 when the Red Rose beat New Zealand 38–21 at Twickenham – a record victory over the All Blacks.

Although an RBS 6 Nations title has so far eluded Lancaster and his team, England once again finished as runners-up in the 2014 tournament and claimed a first Triple Crown success in 11 years.

ANDY FARRELL —
BACKS COACH

A glittering rugby league career with Wigan Warriors and Great Britain brought Farrell five championship titles, four Challenge Cup triumphs and 34 caps. And the 13-man code's loss was union's gain when he signed for Saracens in 2005. After making eight appearances for England, he turned his attention to coaching and first worked with Lancaster as the Saxons won the Churchill Cup in 2010. He enhanced his growing reputation when he steered Saracens to a maiden Premiership crown the following year. Lancaster renewed their working relationship in 2012 after he was appointed interim head coach and, after a brief return to club rugby, Farrell was offered a permanent RFU contract. His work with the Red Rose rapidly earned wider recognition and, in the summer of 2013, he headed to Australia with the British & Irish Lions as assistant coach with responsibility for defence.

GRAHAM ROWNTREE —
FORWARDS COACH

A redoubtable scrummager, Rowntree won 54 England caps over an 11-year Test career that featured two Grand Slams and two World Cup campaigns, as well as three appearances in the front row for the Lions in 2005. He took his first steps in coaching with his beloved Leicester Tigers as an assistant to Pat Howard before he was recruited by the RFU in 2007 as a National Academy Coach. He rose quickly through the ranks, becoming an assistant to former Welford Road team-mate Martin Johnson in the senior England set-up in August 2008. The following year he renewed acquaintances with the Lions, when he was named assistant forwards coach for the tour to New Zealand, and Lancaster retained his services in 2012 when he succeeded Johnson as head coach. In 2013, he was back on the road with the Lions in Australia as assistant coach.

MIKE CATT —
ATTACKING SKILLS COACH

A member of an exclusive group of players to have appeared in two World Cup finals (in 2003 and 2007), Catt was capped 75 times for England between 1994 and 2007, amassing 142 points for the Red Rose. He began his coaching career while still playing for London Irish, becoming the Exiles' attack coach in 2008, and finally hung up his boots after 18 years in 2010. He continued to work with Irish until the summer of 2012, when he toured South Africa with England as backs coach. He was subsequently appointed the RFU's attacking skills coach for England's Elite players.

England captain Katy
Mclean holds the World
Cup aloft after victory
over Canada in the
Women's World Cup
final in France.

WOMEN'S
UGBY WORLD CUP
2014

England's Women in 2014

Since their inaugural Test match in 1987, England's women have experienced some incredible moments, but 2014 was without doubt one of their greatest years ever. Gary Street's team bounced back from the disappointment of losing their opening Six Nations match to France to win the Triple Crown and then, later in the year, became the game's undisputed number one side following their victory over Canada in the final of the World Cup in France.

World Cup Glory

The seventh edition of the Women's World Cup in 2014 saw England desperately hoping to bring to an end an agonizing sequence of three successive defeats in the final and become the world champions for the first time since they had beaten the United States in Cardiff in 1994.

The 20-year drought had been torturous. Three successive appearances in the final, beginning with the 2002 instalment of the tournament, had all climaxed with narrow defeats against New Zealand, and as the Red Roses prepared for battle again in 2014, they did so with both anticipation and excitement.

The road to possible redemption took England over the Channel to France in August. It would ultimately lead Gary Street's side to Paris, where an emotional, cathartic victory over Canada in the final saw the team write a glorious new chapter in the history of the women's game.

Emily Scarratt was one of England's top performers during their triumphant 2014 Women's World Cup campaign in France.

Women's Rugby World Cup

ROUTE TO THE FINAL

With memories of their 13–10 defeat to the Black Ferns in the 2010 final still painfully fresh, the England squad assembled outside Paris in late summer with a simple mission statement. The time had come to relinquish their unwelcome role as perennial runners-up and lift the World Cup. The collective might of France, New Zealand, Ireland and Canada all stood in their way, but fresh from their Six Nations Triple Crown success, the Red Roses were ready.

The stage for the group phase of the tournament was the French National Rugby Centre in the town of Marcoussis. Gary Street's team were drawn in Pool A alongside Canada, Spain and Samoa, and their first target was to ensure they emerged from the group unscathed.

They began their campaign against the Samoans and got off to an explosive start, running in ten tries in a 65–3 demolition of the Pacific Islanders. Worcester wingers Katherine Merchant and Lydia Thompson,

Lichfield scrum-half Natasha Hunt and Thurrock flyer Kay Wilson all scored twice, while Lichfield centre Emily Scarratt scored 20 points. England were up and running.

They were back in action against Spain four days later, and it proved another one-sided clash as the Red Rose crossed the line six times in a 45–5 victory. A brace from Wasps flanker Marlie Packer was the highlight of the second half and England were two for two.

The biggest test of the group still lay ahead, however, in the shape of unbeaten Canada. Street rested captain Katy Mclean for the group decider, keeping faith in Ceri Large at fly-half, and Lichfield No.8 Sarah Hunter retained the captain's armband.

The two teams produced a ferocious tussle. Canada scored the only try of the first half through Karen Paquin in the 14th minute, but two penalties from Scarratt ensured England went in at the break 6–5 up. A second try from the Canucks, from Kayla Mack just four minutes after the restart, saw the Red Roses fall behind once again, but the lead was restored in the 56th minute when Hunter crashed over.

England were on course for victory, but ultimately had to settle for a share of the spoils when Magali Harvey knocked over a late penalty, and the final score stood at 13–13.

The result saw England win Pool A courtesy of their superior points difference to set up a semi-final clash with Ireland, while the Canadians also progressed to the last four as the best group runners-up.

Left: Scrum-half Natasha Hunt scored twice in the group stage victory over Samoa in Marcoussis.

> "If you had said to us at the start of the tournament that we would have the opportunity to play France or Canada in the final then, of course, we would have taken it."

Gary Street

RESULTS

1 AUGUST 2014 (POOL A)
England 65   Samoa 3

5 AUGUST 2014 (POOL A)
England 45   Spain 5

9 AUGUST 2014 (POOL A)
England 13   Canada 13

13 AUGUST 2014 (SEMI-FINAL)
England 40   Ireland 7

LEADING POINTS-SCORERS
(INCLUDING SEMI-FINAL)

1	54	Emily **SCARRATT**	(1t, 7p, 14c)
2	20	Kay **WILSON**	(4t)
=	20	Marlie **PACKER**	(4t)
4	15	Katherine **MERCHANT**	(3t)
5	10	Lydia **THOMPSON**	(2t)
=	10	Natasha **HUNT**	(2t)
7	5	La Toya **MASON**	(1t)
=	5	Danielle **WATERMAN**	(1t)
=	5	Laura **KEATES**	(1t)
=	5	Claire **ALLAN**	(1t)
=	5	Sarah **HUNTER**	(1t)
=	5	Rochelle **CLARK**	(1t)
13	4	Ceri **LARGE**	(2c)

Above: Wing Kay Wilson scores one of England's five tries in their 40–17 defeat of Ireland in the semi-final.

"We know that we've been in a battle," said Hunter. "It was a great game to be involved in. We're delighted to get out of the pool."

England decamped to the Stade Jean-Bouin in Paris for the semi-final. They had beaten Ireland 17–10 in the Six Nations earlier in the year, but the Irish were in form, having recorded a shock victory over New Zealand in the group stage to send the defending champions crashing out of the tournament. Street made six changes in skipper Mclean returning, La Toya Mason getting the nod at scrum-half, Sophie Hemming at prop and Victoria Fleetwood coming in at hooker.

Ireland drew first blood in the French capital when Alison Miller went over in the 17th minute for a converted try, but the score only served to fire up England, and they responded nine minutes later when prop Rochelle Clark muscled her way over the line. Scarratt missed the attempted conversion but, significantly, the Red Rose had found their rhythm.

A Merchant try before half time gave England the lead and, after the break, Street's side were imperious as Wilson and Packer twice breached the Irish defence. When the full-time whistled sounded, England had romped to a 40-7 victory. They were through to the World Cup final for the fourth tournament in a row and found themselves just 80 minutes from glory.

"We felt the scoreboard was fair, because we were clinical in attack and strong in defence," said England coach Street after the Ireland match. "One of our strengths is the amount of experience we have in the squad. To be able to bring players off the bench with 60 caps is a huge bonus, and picking the squad for the final will certainly be a challenge."

Women's Rugby World Cup

THE FINAL

Unbeaten in the group stages and dominant in their last-four dissection of Ireland, England went into their sixth World Cup final with a clean bill of health and with their confidence high. The team refused to shy away from their heart-breaking hat-trick of final defeats in the previous three tournaments, but with a glorious opportunity to atone the disappointment at hand, the Red Roses were in a buoyant mood.

England Rugby

ENG 21
CAN 9

Date: **17 August 2014**
Stadium: **Stade Jean-Bouin, Paris**
Attendance: **20,000**
Referee: **Amy Perrett (Australia)**

It is a potential quirk of any tournament that two teams who have already crossed swords earlier in the competition can do battle again, and so it was at the 2014 World Cup as England found themselves facing a familiar foe in the final.

Canada's 18–16 triumph over France in the semi-final came courtesy of 13 points from impressive wing Magali Harvey, and with memories of their 13–13 draw with the Canucks in the pool stage just nine days earlier still vivid, Gary Street's side knew they were poised for a fierce encounter in the Stade Jean-Bouin.

The head coach made just two changes to the starting XV that had despatched the Irish, recalling Lichfield scrum-half Natasha Hunt in place of La Toya Mason and Marlie Packer, the Wasps flanker, for Alexandra Matthews.

"It was immensely tough to select this team," Street acknowledged before kick-off. "We have 26 players fit and everyone is in a really good place freshness wise, so it was a very difficult call. We have had 27 players play a part in this World Cup experience and with one game to go it is always going to be very tough on those not selected.

"In 2010, we felt a real weight of expectation going into the final and we have learned a lot from that experience. Playing Canada in the pool stages, although it was very tough, was very useful. They really brought their A game to that match and we didn't perform as we wanted to."

There was a 20,000-strong crowd in Paris to watch the final unfold, and it was England who emerged from the early exchanges in the French capital with the upper hand. Two unanswered penalties from the boot of Emily Scarratt established a 6–0 platform before the Red Rose really underlined their superiority with the first try of the match.

It came in the 33rd minute, when second row Tamara Taylor combined with veteran flanker Maggie Alphonsi to create space for Danielle Waterman. It was Taylor's sublime dummy that initially created the space in the midfield and when the lock found Alphonsi, she looked for support. The Canucks' Julianne Zussman surged forward to make the tackle on the England flanker, but Waterman took her exquisitely timed pass safely and the full-back's searing burst of pace took her over in the right-hand corner. A Harvey penalty deep in first-half injury time cut the Canadian arrears, but England headed to the dressing

Above: **Emily Scarratt scored the decisive second try in Paris against Canada to ensure England were crowned world champions.**

Opposite: **England's triumphant players celebrated at the Stade Jean-Bouin after defeating the Canucks in the final.**

"So many great legends that have gone before us haven't won [a World Cup] in an England shirt, and that was for all of them that were here today and for all of the England rugby family."

Katy Mclean

England 21	Canada 9
15 Danielle WATERMAN	15 → Julianne ZUSSMAN
14 → Katherine MERCHANT	14 Magali HARVEY
13 Emily SCARRATT	13 Mandy MARCHAK
12 → Rachael BURFORD	12 Andrea BURK
11 · Kay WILSON	11 → Jessica DOVANNE
10 Katy MCLEAN (c)	10 Emily BELCHOS
9 → Natasha HUNT	9 Elissa ALARIE
1 Rochelle CLARK	1 → Marie-Pier PINAULT-REID
2 → Victoria FLEETWOOD	2 → Kim DONALDSON
3 → Sophie HEMMING	3 → Hilary LEITH
4 Tamara TAYLOR	4 Latoya BLACKWOOD
5 → Jo McGILCHRIST	5 → Maria SAMSON
6 → Marlie PACKER	6 Jacey MURPHY
7 Margaret ALPHONSI	7 Karen PAQUIN
8 Sarah HUNTER	8 Kelly RUSSELL (c)

REPLACEMENTS	REPLACEMENTS
2 ← 16 Emma CROKER	2 ← 16 Laura RUSSELL
5 ← 17 Laura KEATES	3 ← 17 Olivia DEMERCHANT
3 ← 18 Rebecca ESSEX	1 ← 18 Mary Jane KIRBY
6 ← 19 Alexandra MATTHEWS	19 Tyson BEUKEBOOM
9 ← 20 La Toya MASON	5 ← 20 Kayla MACK
12 ← 21 Ceri LARGE	15 ← 21 Julia SUGAWARA
14 ← 22 Claire ALLAN	11 ← 22 Brittany WATERS

SCORES

SCORES

Tries: **Waterman (33)**, **Scarratt (74)**

Con: **Scarratt (75)**

Pens: **Scarratt (11, 25, 60)**

Pens: **Harvey (40, 45, 58)**

room at the break with an 11–3 advantage.

Indiscipline briefly threatened to derail England in the second period as they conceded two penalties, both of which Harvey knocked over, and although they remained the dominant force in the contest, the English lead was now reduced to a precarious two points. A second successful penalty from Scarratt on the hour mark went some way to steadying the nerves, but with the Canucks still within a converted try of going in front, the game was finely poised.

The decisive score came in the 75th minute, and it went to England. Substitute hooker Emma Croker found fellow replacement Rebecca Essex at the front of a lineout on the Canadian 22. The pack drove and, after making two metres, scrum-half Hunt took control. The ball went through the hands of fly-half Katy Mclean and she found the onrushing Scarratt, who came back on the angle and sliced powerfully through the attempted tackles of Jessica Dovanne and then Andrea Burk for the crucial try. The centre converted and, at 21–9, England were firmly on top.

There was no time for a Canadian fightback as Street's team held firm for the remaining five minutes and when the final whistle blew, England were the world champions. Twenty years of World Cup pain had been banished and the party could finally begin.

"All credit to Canada, they were fantastic today, but this group of girls and this group of staff deserve everything that we have got because we have worked so hard for this," said captain Mclean.

IN PROFILE:

Emily Scarratt

The undisputed star of the England's World Cup triumph, Scarratt burst onto the international scene in 2008 when she scored 12 tries in 12 Tests and has gone on to become one of the players now spearheading the new professional era in the women's game.

England Rugby

Position: **Centre/ Full back**

Age: **24**

Height: **1.81m (5'11")**

Weight: **78kg (12st 3lb)**

Caps: **50**

To those who knew Emily Scarratt when she was growing up, her sporting success will come as no surprise. As a teenager she played hockey at county level, rounders for England and, at the age of 16, was offered a US basketball scholarship. That rugby eventually won her affections owed much to the inadvertent intervention of her older brother Joe.

"Joe is three years older and my dad took him down to [local club] Leicester Forest when he was about eight," she said. "I went along with no intention of playing, just for something to do on a Sunday morning. A coach asked if I wanted to have a little pass around and I was pretty much hooked from that point on. It toughens you up, playing with the boys."

For the next seven years, Scarratt played alongside the boys, accepting the inevitable bumps and bruises uncomplainingly. At 12, the club launched a girls' team and, in 2007, aged just 17, she joined Premiership side Lichfield, for whom she still plays her club rugby.

Equally comfortable at full-back or centre, it was not long before Scarratt received a senior England call-up, and her performances for the Red Roses have seen her mature into one of the world game's star turns.

Voted the Rugby Players' Association England Women's Player of the Year in 2013, she has already amassed more than 50 caps for her country and she was both an ever present and the top scorer for Gary Street's side as England claimed the Triple Crown in the 2014 Six Nations.

The defining moment of her career, however, came at the World Cup in France. Scarratt started all five games in the tournament, top scored with 70 points and

her 16 points in the final, including the team's pivotal second try in Paris and three crucial penalties, was the difference between the two sides as England beat Canada 21–9.

The reward for her herculean efforts at the World Cup was the award of a professional contract from the RFU alongside 10 of the country's leading women players. It means Scarratt has relinquished her job as a PE teacher at King Edward's School in Birmingham, but after years of juggling the demands of full-time employment and international rugby, life will be significantly more straightforward in the future.

> "I went along with no intention of playing, just for something to do on a Sunday morning. A coach asked if I wanted to have a little pass around and I was pretty much hooked from that point on. It toughens you up, playing with the boys."
>
> **Emily Scarratt**

"Some tours fell in the school holidays, which was perfect," she said "But some didn't, and you needed to have a very understanding employer. Competing in New Zealand or China could mean a two-week trip away. The school was very accommodating."

King Edward's loss will be England's gain, and with rugby returning to the Olympic Games in Rio in 2016, Scarratt's talents look set to enjoy the greatest stage of them all.

Right: Emily Scarratt of England gets away from an attempted tackle by Nora Stapleton of Ireland during the IRB Women's Rugby World Cup semi-final.

Triple Crown Triumph

Champions on 13 occasions since the inaugural Women's Six Nations Championship in 1996, England went into the 2014 Six Nations in search of their first title since their 2012 Grand Slam.

In 2013, the Red Roses had rested 17 leading players to focus on the Sevens World Cup in Russia later in the year and finished third in the table. However, with their top names back 12 months later, they bounced back in style to clinch a record-breaking 16th Triple Crown.

A 13th Grand Slam narrowly eluded Gary Street's side after they were beaten by the French in Grenoble at the start of the competition, but they responded to the disappointment with wins over Scotland in Aberdeen, defending champions Ireland at Twickenham, Wales at the Twickenham Stoop and against Italy in Lombardy.

England celebrate their Women's Six Nations victory over Wales at the Twickenham Stoop to secure the Triple Crown.

2014 SIX NATIONS TABLE

Pos	Team	P	W	D	L	PF	PA	Tries	PTS
1	France	5	5	0	0	162	21	25	10
2	England	5	4	0	1	145	31	23	8
3	Ireland	5	3	0	2	137	42	20	6
4	Italy	5	3	0	2	57	108	8	4
5	Wales	5	1	0	4	45	88	5	2
6	Scotland	5	0	0	5	5	261	1	0

England
Rugby

2014 Women's Six Nations Championship

England's glorious sequence of three consecutive Grand Slams between 2010 and 2012 had been brought to an abrupt end by Ireland in 2013, and with the Red Roses looking to resolve selection dilemmas, consolidate strategy and build momentum in the crucible of the Six Nations ahead of the World Cup in France later in the year, the 2014 instalment of the championship had an even greater resonance than ever.

There is no better preparation for a tournament than to triumph in the one that immediately precedes it. Confidence can be both infectious and elusive, and as Gary Street readied his troops for the 2014 Six Nations, his eighth as England head coach, he was acutely aware of the importance of a strong performance in the tournament.

And kicking off their championship campaign away to France in early February certainly provided a stern examination of

his side's credentials. *Les Bleus* may not have vanquished England on French soil in a full decade, but they had beaten Street's team 30–20 at Twickenham in 2013 to derail England's own title bid and pave the way for Ireland's championship success.

The annual Anglo-Gallic clash was staged at the Stade des Alpes in Grenoble, and it produced a breathless first half of rugby. The home side were first on the scoreboard when French fly-half Sandrine Agricole landed

Left: **Katy Mclean engages in contact as a trio of Welsh players attempt to stop the England captain.**

a tenth-minute drop goal, but England's riposte came two minutes later when captain Katy Mclean was on target with a penalty. A second penalty from the captain handed the visitors a 6–3 lead, but an Agricole penalty seven minutes before the break saw the teams locked at 6–6 at half time.

It seemed too close to call, but the Red Rose could find no way through a well-marshalled French defence after the interval, while France's hooker and captain Gaëlle Mignot led by example, muscling her way over in the 44th and 64th minutes to seal an 18–6 victory.

England had made the worst possible start to the tournament and Street refused to gloss over the side's frailties in his post-match post mortem.

"This was a disappointing performance in every aspect," the head coach said. "We let ourselves down, while France took their opportunities. We thought we had done our preparations well, but clearly we have not done them well enough. This is a big lesson for us to learn, and we have got to get it right against Scotland next Sunday."

Street's displeasure with the performance was illustrated by his team selection for the game against the Scots in Aberdeen. Only Mclean and the midfield pairing of Rachael Burford and Emily Scarratt survived in the starting XV from the French clash, and the wholesale changes certainly had the desired effect as England ran riot north of the border.

The points deluge began in the seventh minute, when second row Joanna McGilchrist crashed over. The tries – ten more in total – flowed with reassuring regularity from an English perspective, and when referee Christine Bigaran finally put the home side out of their misery, the Red Roses had smashed Scotland 63–0.

"I'm pleased with the win overall," Street said in Aberdeen, in stark contrast to his mood eight days earlier. "Scotland is a difficult place to come, but some of our play today was fantastic, including the play between our backs and forwards. We made mistakes too and that is partly because I made lots of changes to the team, but we know if we can keep playing with that sort of intensity we can still be a threat. Certainly losing to France rallied us on this week. It was a painful result, but we have made amends today to an extent

Right: **Kay Wilson goes over in the corner to score the try that gave England a 12–10 half-time lead against Ireland at Twickenham.**

with this comprehensive victory."

However, the coach's evident satisfaction with his team's display in Aberdeen did not stop him from making seven changes to the England team selected to face Ireland a fortnight later. A complete new front row of Rochelle Clark, Emma Croker and Sophie Hemming was summoned, while flankers Maggie Alphonsi and Hannah Gallagher and No.8 Sarah Hunter formed a revamped back row. Natasha Hunt returned to the side at scrum-half in place of La Toya Mason.

The Irish had thrashed England 25–0 the previous season en route to their first-ever Grand Slam, but the boot would be on the other foot this time round when the two teams reignited their rivalry at Twickenham.

The power of the England scrum provided the platform for opening try at HQ as Hunter picked up and drove over in the eighth minute, and although a try from Ireland scrum-half Larissa Muldoon briefly put the visitors 10–7 in front after an earlier Niamh Briggs penalty, Ireland did not trouble the scoreboard again. England struck again moments before the half-time whistle when a quick switch from right to left saw Scarratt offload intelligently to wing Kay Wilson, who was quick enough to race over at the corner.

Leading 12–10 at the break, the home side were far from safe, but there was to be only one further score at Twickenham in the second period – taken by England's substitute

Left: **Emily Scarratt burst clear of the Welsh defence on her way to scoring one of her two tries in England's 35–3 victory at The Twickenham Stoop.**

flanker Marlie Packer. The Red Roses may have had McGilchrist sin-binned for not releasing, but they held on for a 17–10 triumph that avenged the reverse they had suffered against the Irish the year before. The Triple Crown was now within touching distance, and only Wales could deny Street's team.

An early penalty from Scarratt, who had switched to full-back for the Stoop clash, was scant reward for England's initial dominance, and the Wales defence proved stubbornly resistant to England's attacking overtures until the 26th minute when centres Amber Reed and Rachael Burford combined to create space for Scarratt.

A minute before the break, Wilson extended the advantage, before Scarratt completed her own personal double on the stroke of half time when she scored England's third try. With the visitors only able to muster a Robyn Wilkins penalty in reply, the home side held a comfortable 25–3 lead.

Street emptied the bench in the first 19 minutes of the second half, and it was one of his substitutes, debutant wing Natasha Brennan, who scored the fourth try of the game with her first touch in Test rugby. The ever-present Alphonsi completed the scoring seven minutes from the end and England ran out 35–3 victors.

"We are in a good place heading into the

final weekend and the match against Italy," Street said after England had wrapped up the Triple Crown. "We have a raft of very talented players not in tonight's squad still knocking on the door for consideration.

"I'm really pleased with the energy that the substitutions added. Ceri Large, in particular, made a real impact when she came on in place of captain Katy Mclean, and I was overjoyed for Natasha Brennan, who scored on her international debut at XVs."

England went into the denouement of the Six Nations knowing they could not win the title. They faced the Italians in Rovato on the Sunday afternoon of the final weekend of the championship, but France had crossed swords with Ireland in Pau on the Friday evening and their 19–15 victory saw them complete a Grand Slam. There was nothing more to play for than pride and second place in the final table. Once again Street made wholesale changes to his starting XV, and only wing Katherine Merchant, Scarratt, Clark, Taylor and Alphonsi were retained from the win over the Welsh.

It was not England's most fluent performance of the tournament in the Stadio Giulio e Silvio Pagani, but it was good

RESULTS

1 FEBRUARY 2014 (STADE DES ALPES, GRENOBLE)

France 18   England 6

9 FEBRUARY 2014 (RUBISLAW)

Scotland 0   England 63

22 FEBRUARY 2014 (TWICKENHAM)

England 17   Ireland 10

7 MARCH 2014 (TWICKENHAM STOOP)

England 35   Wales 3

16 MARCH 2014 (GIULIO E SILVIO PAGANI, ROVATO)

Italy 0   England 24

POINTS-SCORERS

1	31	Emily **SCARRATT**	(4t, 1p, 4c)
2	24	Katy **MCLEAN**	(1t, 3p, 5c)
3	10	Amber **REED**	(2t)
=	10	Sarah **HUNTER**	(2t)
=	10	Margaret **ALPHONSI**	(2t)
=	10	Kay **WILSON**	(2t)
7	5	Joanne **McGILCHRIST**	(1t)
=	5	Lydia **THOMPSON**	(1t)
=	5	Claire **PURDY**	(1t)
=	5	Claire **ALLAN**	(1t)
=	5	Sophie **HEMMING**	(1t)
=	5	Hannah **GALLACHER**	(1t)
=	5	Marlie **PACKER**	(1t)
=	5	Natasha **BRENNAN**	(1t)
=	5	Danielle **WATERMAN**	(1t)
=	5	Laura **KEATES**	(1t)

enough to see off the *Azzurri*'s challenge as the visitors scored four tries and prevented their hosts from registering a single point.

Predictably it was the irrepressible Scarratt who got the ball rolling in the 13th minute with the opening try, her fourth of the tournament, and England added a second before the interval courtesy of full-back Danielle Waterman.

Italy's blunt attack unduly failed to trouble England and soon after the restart tighthead prop Laura Keates bundled her way over from close range after a muscular driving maul by the pack. England had to wait until the 70th minute for their fourth try, which came from Reed, and when Scarratt successfully converted it took her personal points tally for the championship to 31, making the Lichfield star the tournament's leading points scorer.

When the final whistle sounded, England were 24–0 winners and had secured the runners-up spot in the table behind the French and ahead of Ireland. It may not have been the Six Nations title Street and his squad had craved, but it was, nonetheless, an encouraging campaign in which they had scored 23 tries in five outings and had propelled England to the World Cup both battle-hardened and bullish.

Above: England's Joanne McGilchrist makes a powerful break against the Italians during the 24–0 victory in Rovato.

"We obviously wanted to win the 6 Nations, but the primary goal is the World Cup this season. What the 6 Nations has allowed us to do is play nearly all of the World Cup squad, try out several different combinations and that is going to stand us in a good stead in five months' time."

Gary Street

IN PROFILE:

Gary Street

As the man who masterminded England's victory over Canada in the final of the 2014 World Cup, Gary Street has played a pivotal role in transforming public perceptions of the women's game.

England Rugby

Position: **Head coach**
Age: **47**

They say good things come to those who wait. Gary Street had to wait seven long and frequently frustrating years to realize his particular dream but, by his own admission, the moment of fulfilment was all the sweeter for the prolonged delay.

A former England Students, Under-18s and Academy coach, Street was appointed the women's head coach in 2007. His first six seasons at the helm brought an incredible five Grand Slams in the Six Nations: England's domination of the European stage was beyond question.

A World Cup crown, however, eluded him. His side did reach the final on home soil in 2010, only to slip to an agonizing 13–10 defeat to New Zealand at the Stoop, a third consecutive defeat to the Black Ferns in the final, and the strong sense of mission unaccomplished remained.

A person of weaker resolve may have been tempted to call it a day, but Street was more determined than ever to win the World Cup, and declined to step aside. The four-year wait for redemption was as painful as it was drawn-out, but when the 2014 tournament in France finally came around, England made no mistake against Canada in the final, beating the Canucks 21–9 to end the Red Roses' patient wait to be crowned champions.

"It's quite surreal and I think I'll wake up in a minute," Street admitted after the final. "It's a pretty amazing feeling, and we're just so proud of everyone involved. It's a really special group, we've been on a long journey, but to have that trophy makes it worthwhile. The support we've had has been amazing and it's a huge relief to be able to deliver."

The win was, of course, a personal triumph for the long-serving former Aston Old Edwardians scrum-half, but the impact of his side's triumph in Paris ultimately went far beyond the mere lifting of an albeit-coveted trophy.

"We had a lovely text from Prince Harry congratulating us and we had a nice message from the Prime Minister too," Street explained. "Things like that were really quite special. We had a nice text from Jonny Wilkinson before the final as well, saying go and win it. So that shows how things have changed."

> "It's a pretty amazing feeling, and we're just so proud of everyone involved. It's a really special group, we've been on a long journey, but to have that trophy makes it worthwhile. The support we've had has been amazing and it's a huge relief to be able to deliver."

Gary Street

That change was indelibly underlined just eight days after the final, when it was announced that 20 of England's leading players were to be handed full-time, central contracts with the RFU for the first time. In lifting the World Cup, Street had won a long-standing personal battle, but he had also helped achieve an even greater victory for the women's game.

Opposite: **Victory in the World Cup final was the culmination of seven years of hard work for England women's head coach Gary Street.**

England
Rugby

England Women Enter the Professional Era

The 2014 World Cup was the end of an era for women's rugby in England. The Red Rose went to the tournament in France as amateurs, but following their glorious triumph in the final, and with the Rugby Sevens at the 2016 Olympics in Rio at the forefront of future planning, it was not long before the RFU took the historic decision to make 11 of England's leading players professional.

The media have always loved tales of plucky amateurs crossing swords with professional opponents and, in the build-up to the World Cup, they voraciously filled countless column inches with stories of England's champions elect, a fascinating assortment of plumbers and police officers, vets and primary school teachers, gardeners and accounts clerks.

England were one of only five squads at the 12-team tournament not to feature professional players in their ranks. It was an anomaly given the outstanding performances of Gary Street's side, and their amateur status certainly made their eventual triumph in the final all the greater.

What was even more incongruous was the unqualified success of the World Cup tournament itself. A capacity crowd of 20,000 filled the Stade Jean-Bouin in Paris to watch England overcome Canada, an estimated two million watched the match on French television and 137 countries broadcast the game around the world. There was nothing amateur about the tournament, except England.

The time had come to move the women's game to a new level and, eight days after the World Cup final, the RFU announced it was awarding 20 full-time central contracts, 11 of which went to members of the World Cup-winning squad, including captain Katy Mclean, top scorer Emily Scarratt and leading try scorer Marlie Packer. For the first time in England, the players were to be paid and resignation letters were hastily typed to former employers.

The contracts were primarily designed to allow the England Sevens side to prepare full time for the upcoming 2014–15 IRB Women's Sevens World Series. England finished fourth as amateurs in 2013–14 and a repeat performance, or better, will confirm Team GB's qualification for the Olympics in Rio.

The new deals also stipulated that the players would be made available for the Red Roses' 15-a-side team. It was an announcement that had ramifications for both formats of the sport.

Below: **Captain Kay Mclean was one of the 11 England players to be awarded a full-time contract by the RFU.**

Above: **Wing Katherine Merchant was rewarded for a series of superb displays at the World Cup for England.**

Above right: **Emily Scarratt will now be able to focus on her rugby career full-time after the RFU's historic decision to offer contracts to women players.**

"This is fantastic news for the sport and exactly what we need as an England squad to continue to be at the top of our sport on a global scale," said Mclean. "I am extremely excited about this new challenge and where this full-time programme can take us as an England team."

The newly-contracted players will train five days a week at Twickenham and at the Surrey Sports Park in Guildford, where they will receive strength and conditioning, medical and nutritional support. The programme will be run by the RFU's Head of Women's Performance Nicola Ponsford and England Women's Sevens head coach Simon Middleton.

"We are delighted to be able to offer a full-time Sevens programme for next season," Ponsford said after the RFU's decision had been confirmed. "We are really excited by the opportunity and feel that this will enable us to compete on a global level. The inclusion of Sevens in the Olympics has meant that a significant number of sides we are competing against have been full time for a year or more.

"We have been planning to do this for some time, but we needed to make sure that we could focus on the XVs Rugby World Cup while also ensuring we had the building blocks in place to guarantee that a full-time programme is effective. With two years to go until the 2016 Olympic Games, we felt this was the right time to move forward."

The new contracts will be reviewed annually and see England follow the Netherlands, Australia, New Zealand, Ireland, South Africa, Canada, the United States, Russia and Spain in awarding their Sevens players professional status.

The 11 players from the World Cup campaign to go full time were: McLean, Scarratt, Packer, Claire Allan, Rachael Burford, Natasha Brennan, Heather Fisher, Danielle Waterman, Natasha Hunt, Alexandra Matthews, and Kay Wilson. They were joined on the RFU pay roll by Richmond quartet Francesca Matthews, Joanne Watmore, Abigail Chamberlain and Alice Richardson, Saracens pair Leanne Riley and Sarah McKenna, Michaela Staniford from Wasps, Bristol's Amy Wilson-Hardy and Thurrock's Emily Scott.

IRB JUNIOR

WINN

England's jubilant Under-20 side celebrate after winning the IRB Junior World Championship in New Zealand at Eden Park, Auckland, New Zealand.

RLD CHAMPIO
ERS 20

The Next Generation

If the success of a Test team can be gauged by the number of talented young players coming through its junior ranks, the future of the England side is bright indeed. The Red Rose has rarely boasted such a pool of outstanding youngsters, and the recent exploits of the England Under-20 team in New Zealand suggest that many of the new generation will be ready to graduate to Stuart Lancaster's senior squad sooner rather than later.

England Conquer the World Again

There's an old sporting adage that it's harder to make a successful defence of a title than it is to win it for the first time. Reigning champions are there to be dethroned, and that is exactly the position England Under-20 side found themselves in as they headed to New Zealand for the 2014 IRB Junior World Championship.

Nick Walshe's team had broken New Zealand and South Africa's five-year monopoly of the trophy in 2013 following their victory over Wales in the final in France. It was a stunning success that helped ease the heartbreak of the defeats they had suffered in three previous final appearances, but 12 months after their maiden triumph, the young Red Rose had it all to do again.

The weight of expectation, however, only seemed to galvanize England's youngsters, as they swept aside all challengers in New Zealand to claim the IRB crown for a second successive year after a dramatic 21–20 final win over the Springboks in Auckland. England were the world champions again, and captain Maro Itoje became the second proud young Englishman, after Jack Clifford in 2013, to lift the coveted trophy.

England captain Maro Itoje (right) and Callum Braley are all smiles as they hold the IRB Junior World Championship trophy in Auckland.

IRB Junior World Championship

ROUTE TO THE FINAL

England arrived in New Zealand in June for the seventh instalment of the IRB Junior World Championship having been drawn with Australia, Argentina and Italy in the pool stages. The young Red Rose had lost in the group phase to the Springboks in 2013, but still went on to be crowned champions. This time round, Nick Walshe and his team wanted to make sure they qualified for the semi-finals with an untarnished record.

England began the defence of their title with a Pool A match against Italy, and if there were any nerves in the ranks, they were quickly dispelled. Walshe's team made short work of the *Azzurri* in Pukekohe, running in nine tries, the first coming as early as the 12th minute, through Nathan Earle. The young Saracens flyer completed his hat-trick eight minutes into the second half, while braces from No.8 James Chisholm and flanker Gus Jones compounded Italy's misery. By the time the final whistle blew, England had posted an impressive 63–3 victory.

The team were back in action four days later, against the Junior Wallabies in Auckland, and the young Australians provided a far sterner examination of England's credentials in a match that was delicately poised at 24–17 to the Red Rose at half time, despite two tries from Saracens scrum-half Henry Taylor. England started the second half with plenty of work still to do, but they finally quelled the Wallaby challenge when Earle raced over midway through the half for his second try of the game, and England ran out 38–24 winners.

The Red Rose were now within touching distance of the semi-finals, but they had to overcome a major scare in their final Pool A clash against Argentina before reaching the last four. The wet and windy conditions inside the QBE Stadium in Auckland made the expansive rugby England had played in the first two games impossible, and as they struggled, the Red Rose came within

a whisker of defeat. The first half turned out to be a battle of the kickers, with Northampton fly-half Sam Olver knocking over three penalties to Pumas skipper Patricio Fernandez's two. England led 9–6 at the break.

The first try of the contest went to England, when wing George Catchpole went over in the 54th minute, and although Olver missed the conversion, Walshe's side were 14–9 up. Disaster struck, however, when substitute prop Harry Rudkin was shown a yellow card midway through the half and with just one minute of his sin-

Above: Harry Sloan centre Harry Sloan opened the try-scoring for England Under-20s in their 42–15 victory over Ireland in the semi-final.

Opposite: Wing Nathan Earle scored a hat-trick in England's 63–3 victory over the Italians in the opening pool match at Pukekohe.

bin remaining, Argentina took advantage of their numerical advantage to score a converted try from centre Emiliano Boffelli.

England trailed by two points and could not find a way back into the match until the 79th minute, when Olver stepped forward to slot his fourth successful penalty to seal a dramatic 17–16 win and set up a last-four clash with Ireland.

"The conditions were extremely tough, but it was the same for both teams and we're just pleased to get the win," Walshe admitted after the game. "We know that we can play better, and we'll have to up our game for the semi-final. We're relishing the opportunity to play Ireland. They've had a good competition so far and it will be an interesting game."

Walshe made a total of 11 changes to his side to tackle the Irish, with skipper and second row Maro Itoje, wings Howard Packman and Earle among those returning to the fray. There was also an entirely new front row, in the shape of Danny Hobbs-Awoyemi, Tom Woolstencroft and Paul Hill.

The return of England's frontline players certainly paid dividends in the QBE Stadium, as the expected close battle with Ireland failed to materialize and the game was effectively over by half time. Centre Harry Sloan sparked the Red Rose's first-half blitz with an eighth-minute try, and he was followed over the line in quick succession by Hobbs-Awoyemi, Packman and Woolstencroft as Walshe's team raced into a 34–3 lead at the break.

Ireland responded with two tries after the restart, but a drop-goal from Packman and a fifth England try, through Jones, ensured that there was to be no heroic fightback from the team in green, and England went on to complete a comprehensive 42–15 victory to secure their place in the final.

"It feels just as special this year as it did last," said Walshe after his team had reached a second successive final. "South Africa will provide a real test for us, but we're excited. It doesn't get much bigger. We're pleased with how we played, particularly in that first half. We challenged the guys to start well and they delivered. Ireland were physical and caused us problems, but we dealt with them well."

---

2 JUNE 2014, PUKEKOHE (POOL A)

England 63   Italy 3

Tries: Earle (12, 46, 48); Jones (21, 58); Chisholm (34, 51); Burns (66); Catchpole (74)

Cons: Olver (22, 47, 49, 52, 59); Burns (67)

Pens: Olver (3, 9)   Pen: Buscema (7)

---

6 JUNE 2014, AUCKLAND (POOL A)

England 38   Australia 24

Tries: Taylor (12, 18); Earle (31, 62); Jones (43)   Tries: Kellaway (5, 34); McIntyre (48)

Cons: Burns (13, 19, 32, 44, 63)   Cons: McIntyre (6, 49); Horwitz (35)

Pen: Burns (8)   Pen: McIntyre (26)

---

10 JUNE 2014, AUCKLAND (POOL A)

England 17   Argentina 16

Try: Catchpole (54)   Try: Boffelli (70)

  Con: Fernandez (70)

Pens: Olver (4, 21, 25, 79)   Pens: Fernandez (11, 24, 42)

---

15 JUNE 2014, AUCKLAND (SEMI-FINAL)

England 42   Ireland 15

Tries: Sloan (8); Hobbs-Awoyemi (21); Packman (27); Woolstencroft (33); Jones (54)   Tries: Ringrose (50); Wooton (68)

Cons: Burns (9, 22, 28, 34)   Con: Byrne (50)

Pens: Burns (4, 12)   Pen: Byrne (19)

Drop: Packman (48)

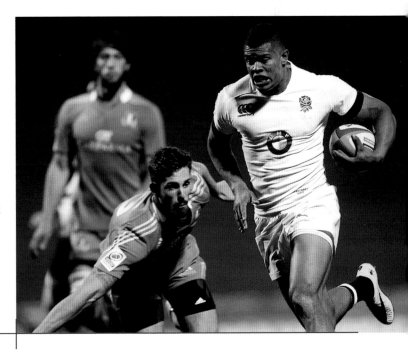

IRB Junior World Championship

THE FINAL

Four wins from four propelled England into the IRB Junior World Championship final at the iconic Eden Park in commanding style, but they would have to overcome the formidable challenge of 2012 champions South Africa if they were to retain their title. The Baby Boks had beaten the Red Rose 31–24 in the 2013 tournament and Nick Walshe's team could ill afford a repeat performance in Auckland.

England Rugby

ENG 21
RSA 20

Date: **20 June 2014**
Stadium: **Eden Park, Auckland, New Zealand**
Referee: **Ben O'Keeffe (New Zealand)**

England's explosive performance against Ireland in the semi-final ensured Walshe had few selection dilemmas ahead of the final. With a fully fit squad to choose from, the coach was clear on his strongest side and named an unchanged team to take on the Springboks.

It meant there were two survivors from the starting XV that had triumphed over Wales in the final 12 months earlier – inside-centre Harry Sloan and blindside flanker

Ross Moriarty – while prop Danny Hobbs-Awoyemi and centre Henry Purdy were both on the bench in Auckland as they had been in 2013 in France.

"South Africa will be a difficult challenge, but we're focusing on ourselves," Walshe said before the match. "We're putting a real emphasis on performing for the full 80 minutes. We feel we have played well in patches throughout the tournament, but we want to see a complete performance.

"What I really wanted the team to do was to gain the respect of the New Zealanders in their own backyard by playing good rugby and being very good ambassadors for England on and off the field. I think there's a massive respect now. The future of English rugby is really, really bright."

The early exchanges at Eden Park were both muscular and ferocious, but the greasy conditions made it difficult for both sides to create chances, and there was no score until Springbok fly-half and captain Handré Pollard landed a 14th-minute penalty. His opposite number, Billy Burns, levelled for England three minutes later.

The first try of the match went to South Africa. England knocked on and Pollard pounced, delivering a perfectly weighted chip before centre Jesse Kriel won the ensuing foot race for the score, which his fly-half duly converted.

A monster penalty from inside his own half from full-back Aaron Morris reduced

Left: **Replacement flanker Joel Conlon, scorer of England's all-important second try, celebrates in the IRB Junior World Championship final against South Africa in Auckland.**

"It was an unbelievable effort in the end. South Africa were coming at us five yards from the line, and the boys just defended it. Just unbelievable bravery and courage; and I'm so proud of them."

Nick Walshe, England coach

England 21		South Africa 20	
15	Aaron MORRIS	15	Warrick GELANT
14	Howard PACKMAN	14	Dan KRIEL
13	Nick TOMPKINS	13	Jesse KRIEL
12	Harry SLOAN	12 →	Andre ESTERHUIZEN
11	Nathan EARLE	11	Sergeal PETERSEN
10	Billy BURNS	10	Handre POLLARD (c)
9	Henry TAYLOR	9	JP SMITH
1 →	Danny HOBBS-AWOYEMI	1 →	Thomas DU TOIT
2 →	Tom WOOLSTENCROFT	2 →	Corniel ELS
3	Paul HILL	3 →	Dayan VAN DER WESTHUIZEN
4	Maro ITOJE (c)	4	JD SCHICKERLING
5	Charlie EWELS	5	Nico Janse VAN RENSBURG
6	Ross MORIARTY	6 →	Jacques VERMEULEN
7 →	Gus JONES	7	Cyle BRINK
8	James CHISHOLM	8	Aidon DAVIS

REPLACEMENTS		REPLACEMENTS	
2 ←	16 Jack WALKER	2 ←	16 Joseph DWEBA
1 ←	17 Alex LUNDBERG	1 ←	17 Pierre SCHOEMAN
	18 Biyi ALO	3 ←	18 Wilco LOUW
	19 Hayden THOMPSON-STRINGER		19 Victor SEKEKETE
7 ←	20 Joel CONLON	6 ←	20 Jean Luc DU PREEZ
	21 Callum BRALEY		21 Zee MKHABELA
	22 Sam OLVER		22 Jean Luc DU PLESSIS
	23 Henry PURDY	12 ←	23 Duhan VAN DER MERWE

SCORES	SCORES
Tries: **Earle (39), Conlon (52)**	Tries: **J Kriel (20, 64)**
Con: **Burns (53)**	Cons: **Pollard (21, 65)**
Pens: **Burns (17, 44), Morris (37)**	Pens: **Pollard (14, 46)**

the deficit, and Walshe's team went in front moments before half-time. A brilliant break from centre Nick Tompkins opened the Baby Boks' defence and although he was dragged down a metre short of the line, the ball was recycled quickly and Nathan Earle was on hand to ghost outside Sergeal Petersen to notch up his sixth try of the tournament. England were 11–10 in front at the break, and the final hung in the balance.

An exchange of penalties early in the second half between Burns and Pollard did little to change the complexion of the contest but, crucially, it was the Red Rose who scored the next try. Good work from pack in the 52nd minute saw a driving maul move inexorably towards the South African line, and Exeter flanker Joel Conlon was in the right place at the right time to touch down. Burns added the two extra points and England found themselves eight points clear.

The Springboks' challenge was not spent, however, and, 12 minutes later, an incursion from wing Duhan van der Merwe created enough space for Jesse Kriel to score his second try of the game to set alarm bells ringing in the England camp. Pollard was on target with the extras and the Red Rose now held a precarious 21–20 lead.

Walshe's side barely got out of their own half in the final 15 minutes. They had to repel a succession of Baby Boks attacks and also watch an attempted Pollard drop-goal sail a fraction wide, but when New Zealand referee Ben O'Keeffe signalled full time, the Red Rose had done just enough to wrap up a 21–20 triumph to become the IRB Junior World Cup champions for a second successive time.

"It doesn't feel real at the moment," admitted captain Maro Itoje after the game. "It's something I dreamt of and I am so happy to be able to lift the trophy. This has been a fantastic tournament for us. Our boys have worked so hard and we got our just desserts. We believed if we stayed true to our principles, we would do well, and we did, we won.

"We have got a fantastic squad and coaching team and we're all so proud. This shows the club Academies are doing their work; that the RFU Academy and their personal development are working. Long may it continue."

IN PROFILE:

Maro Itoje

The captain of the all-conquering England side crowned junior world champions in New Zealand in 2014, 20-year-old Maro Itoje is a hugely talented second row with a bright future, both in the engine room on the pitch, and in the classroom off it.

England Rugby

Position: **Second row/ back row**

Age: **20**

Height: **1.95m**

Weight: **110kg**

Representative teams: **England U18s, U19s, U20s**

Unlike many of his peers, Maro Itoje is a young man who actually loves to do his homework. It's a trait that has already seen the Saracens Academy lock enjoy a meteoric rise up the rugby ranks, and one that also seems destined to propel him to academic success.

Itoje is currently studying for a politics degree at the University of London's School of Oriental and African Studies. Balancing his embryonic professional career with his degree work would be challenging enough, but the youngster is equally studious when it comes to his rugby education.

"I love it when you do your homework on the opposition's weakness in the week leading up to a game, then, when you play the game, you see what you've been studying unfold," he said. "I love it when you get it right. It shows that hard work pays off."

Itoje has certainly learned from the very best at Saracens, and is quick to pay tribute to the guidance of former England captain Steve Borthwick on his rapid development. Borthwick is now in Japan working as an assistant coach with the national side, but before he left England he was a major influence on his young team-mate.

"When I first came down to Saracens he was captain of England, and I could barely speak because I was so nervous," Itoje said. "I was lucky enough to dissect some of his knowledge, in terms of a young second-row growing up; he's the greatest lineout mind I've met. Having such a close experience of watching how he worked, I think I learned a lot."

With such an education, it is hardly surprising Itoje enjoyed such a stellar year in 2014. He was an ever present throughout the Under-20 Six Nations campaign, scoring a try in all five of the Red Rose's fixtures to earn himself the accolade of England Player of the Tournament. In May, he made his Premiership bow for Saracens against Leicester at Welford Road.

Then, of course, there was the glorious IRB Junior World Championship campaign. Itoje had assumed the captaincy midway through the Six Nations after an injury to Bristol scrum-half Callum Braley, and he retained the armband as England swept aside all challengers in New Zealand to make a successful defence of their IRB title, beating South Africa in the final in Auckland.

> "I love it when you do your homework on the opposition's weakness in the week leading up to a game, then, when you play the game, you see what you've been studying unfold."
>
> **Maro Itoje**

The role of captain is relatively new to him, but the youngster already has a clear philosophy on what the job should entail.

"I like to think I don't talk too much," he said. "I like to think that I get the right balance. From the leaders I've seen in my playing career through school and club and at Saracens, I always felt that it's not always the dog that barks the loudest that says the right thing. I try to say things at the right time with the right level of emotion."

Opposite: England Under-20 captain Maro Itoje has a bright future ahead of him for club (Saracens) and country.

England scrum-half James Rodwell looks to get a pass away from the back of a ruck in a match against New Zealand.

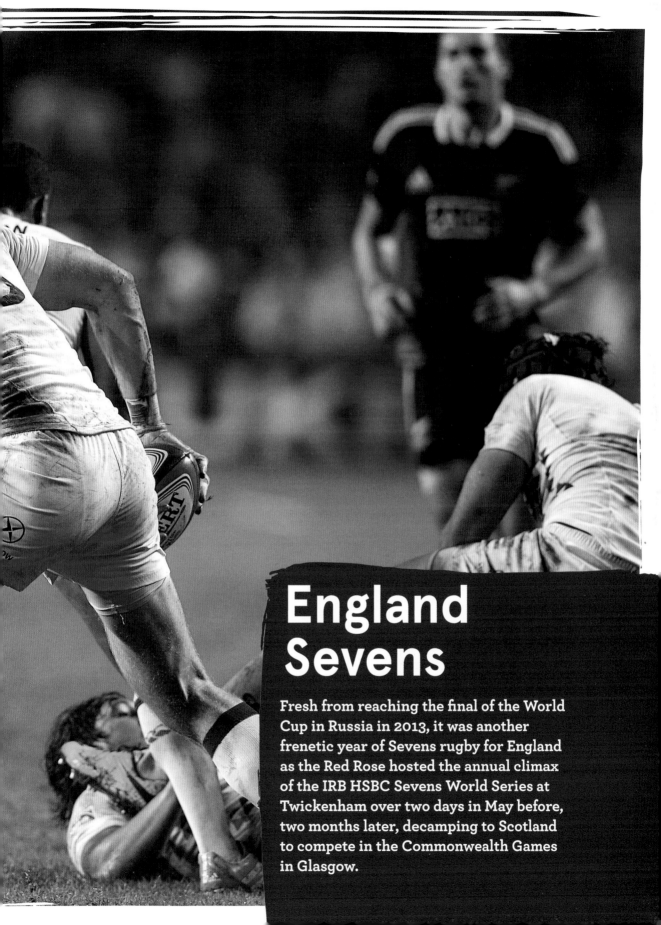

England Sevens

Fresh from reaching the final of the World Cup in Russia in 2013, it was another frenetic year of Sevens rugby for England as the Red Rose hosted the annual climax of the IRB HSBC Sevens World Series at Twickenham over two days in May before, two months later, decamping to Scotland to compete in the Commonwealth Games in Glasgow.

HSBC Sevens World Series 2013–14

The 15th instalment of the World Series was one of evolution and change for England following the RFU's appointment of a new head coach, Simon Amor, and his subsequent decision to install the prolific Tom Mitchell as the side's new captain midway through the eight-month campaign.

A veteran of six successful seasons on the Sevens circuit, the IRB World Sevens Player of the Year in 2004 and a silver medallist with England at the 2006 Commonwealth Games, Amor's CV spoke for itself, and although he could not guide the team to a maiden IRB title, it was a campaign that showed significant improvement after the Red Rose's disappointing six-place finish the previous year.

Mitchell, who finished as the Series' top scorer with 358 points (an incredible 98 clear of his closest rival), enjoyed an outstanding year, and he succeeded Tom Powell as skipper ahead of the USA Sevens in Las Vegas in January.

Dan Norton scored 27 tries during the course of the season; a haul that took the Red Rose flyer to a total of 164 in his spectacular Sevens career since making his debut in Wellington in 2009 and to fifth on the all-time IRB try-scoring list.

Captain Tom Mitchell was in prolific form for England during the 2013–14 World Sevens Series.

England
Rugby

HSBC Sevens World Series

The 2013–14 HSBC Sevens World Series took England to five continents over eight months as they began the countdown to rugby's reintroduction to the Rio de Janeiro 2016 Olympic Games. Five semi-final appearances underlined the Red Rose's growing consistency under Simon Amor's new regime, while the highlight of their campaign came in March, when the side fought their way through to the final of the iconic Hong Kong Sevens.

England headed Down Under for the season-opening Gold Coast event in October with a renewed sense of purpose after their superb displays at the Sevens World Cup in Moscow four months earlier. And the side's reborn confidence was very much in evidence in Australia, with an encouraging third-place finish.

Their commanding 26–12 defeat of Fiji in the Cup quarter-finals set up a last-four meeting with the All Blacks, and although they went down 14–5 to the reigning champions, the Red Rose finished the tournament on a spectacular high, destroying the Springboks 47–0 in the third-place play-off game, with two tries apiece from James Rodwell, Phil Burgess and Dan Bibby.

"Playing on the second day there was a real step-up and it's important to see we're making steps forward," said Amor after his first event as head coach. "To finish third was a good reward for all the effort the boys put in."

England backed up their performance on the Gold Coast in Dubai the following month by progressing to the semi-finals once again. South Africa gained revenge for their mauling in Australia with a 26–12 win in the last four, but the reverse did little to detract from the solid start Amor's charges had made to the series.

The only significant blemish on England's record in 2013–14 came at the South Africa Sevens in December, when they lost to both Argentina and Samoa in the group stages in Port Elizabeth and failed to qualify for the Cup competition. There was, though, the consolation of a triumph in the Bowl final, after they beat the Wallabies 28–19 in the Nelson Mandela Bay Stadium.

The New Year saw England return to the fray in the USA with a new captain after Amor decided to hand the armband to playmaker Tom Mitchell, who succeeded Sevens stalwart Tom Powell. It was a bold move to appoint the 24-year-old in place of the more experienced Powell, but it was one that would pay dividends as the Series unfolded.

"Being named captain is a huge honour,"

Left: **Jeff Williams takes a selfie with the 2014 USA Sevens plate after England's 26–24 defeat of Australia in the final at Sam Boyd Stadium, Las Vegas, USA**

Right: **Tom Powell's try was not enough to stop England slipping to defeat against New Zealand in the final of the Hong Kong Sevens.**

Mitchell said ahead of the action in Las Vegas. "Not coming through the England age groups, I've been really fortunate to be involved and to get where I am now. It's a big task, but I feel confident. I've been in the squad for two years, and although I'm not a shouter, I've learned to voice my opinions more."

The new skipper took the Red Rose to the quarter-finals of the Cup in America. They fell to the All Blacks in the last eight, but Mitchell led from the front in the Sam Boyd Stadium in the Plate final, scoring one of his side's four tries and landing three conversions to seal a thrilling 26–24 win over the Wallabies.

In February, the squad were in New Zealand for the Wellington Sevens and there was a return to form as England toppled South Africa and Wales in the group stages on day one before they convincingly despatched Samoa 21–5 in the quarter-finals 24 hours later. The Kiwis once again ended English hopes in a one-sided semi-final, but after failing to reach the last four in South Africa and America, it was nonetheless a morale-boosting two days.

Defeat to the All Blacks was becoming a frustratingly recurrent theme for England in the series, but Amor's side did not have to wait long for the opportunity to exact their revenge, finally emerging victorious when the two sides met again in the Japan Sevens in March.

Having safely negotiated their pool, England beat Canada in the quarter-finals, but their loss to the Springboks in the next stage ensured they would play New Zealand in the third-place play-off in the Chichibunomiya Stadium.

The game initially seemed to be following a depressingly familiar script as the Kiwis outscored England two tries to one in the first half to establish a 12–7 lead at the turnaround, but the Red Rose came storming back after the restart, and scores from Jack Clifford and Burgess, both converted by Mitchell, wrapped up a cathartic 21–12 triumph.

Buoyed by the result, England headed to the famed Hong Kong Sevens in search of a first final appearance since 2006. They successfully edged past South Africa in the quarter-finals thanks to Clifford's second-half try, and sent Fiji packing after a 17–7 victory in the semis, courtesy of scores from Powell and Marcus Watson and seven points from the boot of Mitchell.

New Zealand lay in wait in the final in Hong Kong, and although a Mitchell try just before half time ensured England were only 14–7 adrift at the break, they were unable to contain the Kiwis in the second period and eventually succumbed to a 24–7 loss.

Amor had captained England the last time they had reached the final eight years earlier, beating Fiji to take the title, and although his side were unable to emulate that feat, the head coach insisted he was happy with their progress.

"I'm incredibly proud of the squad," he said. "To play all three of the big teams on one day, with seven of the players making their Hong Kong debut, is a big achievement. We have made so much progress in recent weeks and months, but unfortunately we weren't quite good enough in that final game. We didn't get some of our decision-making quite right, but that's just a reflection of where we are in terms of our learning curve.

"You get so few opportunities to play in front of 40,000 with an atmosphere as incredible as it is here, and I thought the courage and the way the guys played for the shirt and their country and really fought together throughout the weekend, was just outstanding. It says so much about them as a group. We'll keep on building and, hopefully, next year we can go one stage further."

The Series decamped to Europe for the final two events on the schedule. England exited the Scotland Sevens at the Cup quarter-final stage at the hands of Fiji, but shrugged off the disappointment to beat Australia en route to a 26–5 victory over Kenya in the Plate final in Glasgow.

The climax of the season saw England run out in the reassuringly familiar surroundings of Twickenham for the London Sevens in May, and although they were unable to supply a triumph in the Cup final that the home support desperately craved, there was still cause for considerable celebration.

The highlight came on day one in the group stages. England had already dismissed Wales and Argentina and faced their nemesis in the shape of New Zealand in the final pool game. The Kiwis led 7–5 after the opening ten minutes, but England got their noses in front early in the second half when New Zealand's Tim Mikkelson was sin-binned for an illegal tackle, and Mitchell scored a try with a sublime chip and chase while the Red Rose enjoyed a numerical advantage. The All Blacks responded with a Bryce Heem try to level the scores at 12–12, but the final word went to captain Mitchell after England were awarded a penalty for an infringement at a ruck. His effort turned out to be the last play

Left: **Tom Mitchell proved an inspirational choice as the new captain of the England Sevens side.**

of the match and Twickenham erupted when his kick sailed through the uprights to secure a 15–12 victory.

"The crowd was absolutely incredible," said Amor. "I've never seen a Sevens game like that, with 'Swing Low, Sweet Chariot' being sung around the ground with two minutes to go. That lifted the team at a critical moment, and I'm really glad the players made that connection with the crowd and that they responded to the players in turn. They have worked very hard over the past few weeks and it paid off. It was pleasing, but this is only day one – nothing's won on day one, and we've got a massive game against France tomorrow."

The French game at HQ was another cliff-hanger and was only settled 19–17 in England's favour with a Burgess try late in the second half. Victory set up a Cup semi-final clash against Australia later in the day. It would prove the proverbial game of two halves: the Wallabies ran in three first-half tries, before England came roaring back in the second period with scores from Mitchell and Norton. However, the home side had left themselves with too much to do, and it was the Australians who celebrated at full time with a 15–12 victory.

The Twickenham faithful were only briefly downcast, however, as their side signed off with a thrilling 26–19 victory over Fiji in the third-place play-off game, scoring four tries through Mitchell, Howard Packman, Mat Turner and Rodwell to end the World Series on a high and underline the side's potential ahead of the 2014–15 campaign.

RESULTS

GOLD COAST SEVENS (12–13 OCTOBER 2013)

England 54	Spain 7	(Pool B)
England 26	France 12	(Pool B)
England 14	South Africa 22	(Pool B)
England 26	Fiji 12	(Cup QF)
England 5	New Zealand 14	(Cup SF)
England 47	South Africa 0	(3/4 Playoff)

DUBAI SEVENS (29–30 OCTOBER 2013)

England 47	Canada 7	(Pool C)
England 28	United States 5	(Pool C)
England 21	Fiji 26	(Pool C)
England 33	Wales 12	(QF Cup QF)
England 12	South Africa 26	(Cup SF)
England 14	New Zealand 17	(3/4 Playoff)

SOUTH AFRICA SEVENS (7–8 DECEMBER 2013)

England 14	Samoa 24	(Pool D)
England 35	Zimbabwe 7	(Pool D)
England 19	Argentina 21	(Pool D)
England 19	Scotland 7	(Shield QF)
England 33	United States 14	(Bowl SF)
England 28	Australia 19	(Bowl Final)

USA SEVENS (24–25 JANUARY 2014)

England 19	Samoa 22	(Pool C)
England 54	Portugal 0	(Pool C)
England 43	Uruguay 5	(Pool C)
England 7	New Zealand 24	(Cup QF)
England 21	France 12	(Plate SF)
England 26	Australia 24	(Plate Final)

NEW ZEALAND SEVENS (7–8 FEBRUARY 2014)

England 36	Portugal 7	(Pool A)
England 21	Wales 7	(Pool A)
England 19	South Africa 5	(Pool A)
England 21	Samoa 5	(Cup QF)
England 0	New Zealand 31	(Cup SF)
England 7	Fiji 14	(3/4 Playoff)

JAPAN SEVENS (22–23 MARCH 2014)

England 36	Scotland 0	(Pool D)
England 29	Spain 0	(Pool D)
England 24	Australia 21	(Pool D)
England 14	Canada 10	(Cup QF)
England 0	South Africa 17	(Cup SF)
England 21	New Zealand 12	(3/4 Playoff)

HONG KONG SEVENS (28–29 MARCH 2014)

England 19	Argentina 12	(Pool C)
England 21	Portugal 7	(Pool C)
England 14	Canada 12	(Pool C)
England 14	South Africa 7	(Cup QF)
England 17	Fiji 10	(Cup SF)
England 7	New Zealand 26	(Cup Final)

SCOTLAND SEVENS (3–4 MAY 2014)

England 21	France 5	(Pool B)
England 33	Japan 24	(Pool B)
England 7	Canada 7	(PoolB)
England 12	Fiji 14	(Cup SF)
England 21	Australia 7	(Plate SF)
England 26	Kenya 5	(Plate Final)

LONDON SEVENS (11–12 MAY 2014)

England 14	Wales 10	(Pool A)
England 31	Argentina 5	(Pool A)
England 15	New Zealand 12	(Pool A)
England 19	France 17	(Cup QF)
England 12	Australia 15	(Cup SF)
England 26	Fiji 19	(3/4 Playoff)

"I have never seen a Sevens game like that, with 'Swing Low, Sweet Chariot' being sung around the ground with two minutes to go. That lifted the team at a critical moment."

Simon Amor, head coach

Marcus Watson in action for England at the 2014 Commonwealth Games in Glasgow.

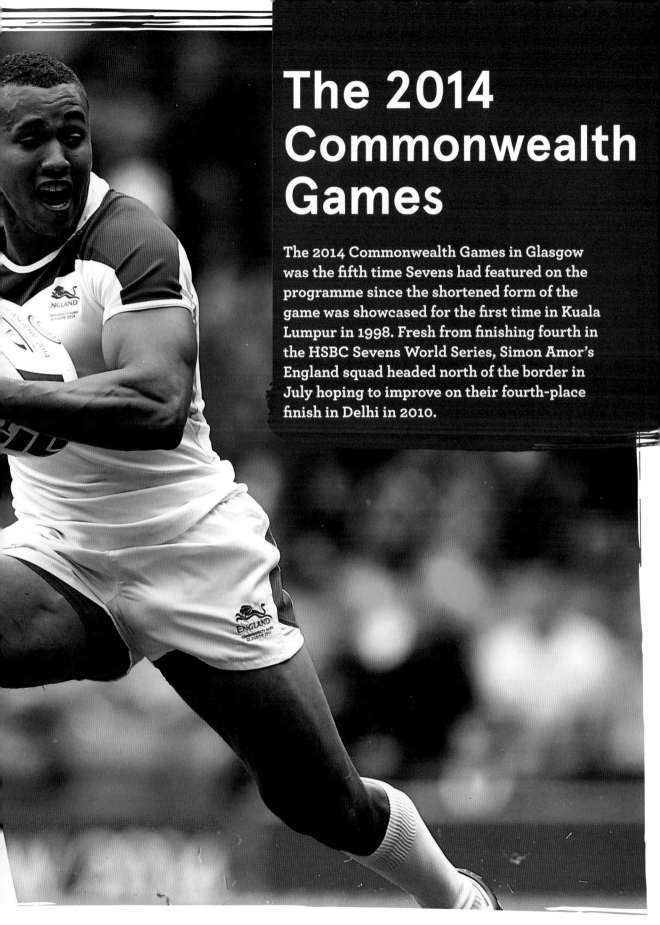

The 2014 Commonwealth Games

The 2014 Commonwealth Games in Glasgow was the fifth time Sevens had featured on the programme since the shortened form of the game was showcased for the first time in Kuala Lumpur in 1998. Fresh from finishing fourth in the HSBC Sevens World Series, Simon Amor's England squad headed north of the border in July hoping to improve on their fourth-place finish in Delhi in 2010.

England triumph in Plate Final

The success of the London Olympics 2012 brought added excitement to the Commonwealth Games, as a second multisport event to be hosted in Britain within two years. Seven of the world's top eight Sevens nations were in action at Ibrox Stadium in pursuit of a coveted medal. It would have been a full house of eight had Fiji's reinstatement to the Commonwealth been ratified in time, but the sad exclusion of the Fijians aside, it was a world-class line-up and a superb advert for the game. That England ultimately fell short, exiting the competition at the quarter-final stage following an agonizingly narrow defeat to Samoa, reflected the quality of the opposition, and with Sevens rugby set to return to the Olympics in Rio in 2016, the sport will be looking to build on the class of rugby showcased in Glasgow. There was, however, consolation for Simon Amor's young team in the shape of victory over Wales in the Plate Final. The morale-boosting result may not have been enough to earn them a medal, but finishing on a win allowed England to show what they are capable of and to thank the crowd for their incredible support across the weekend.

Marcus Watson takes on twin tacklers Luke Morgan (right) and Gareth Davies in the Commonwealth Games Rugby Sevens Plate Final at Ibrox Stadium, which England went on to win 17–15.

The 2014 Commonwealth Games

DAY ONE

The 2010 Commonwealth Games in Delhi had seen England drawn against Australia, Sri Lanka and Uganda in the pool matches and the men in white had beaten all three before going on to be denied a bronze medal after a heart-breaking 17–14 loss to the Springboks in the third-place play-off game. Four years later, they faced the same pool opponents, and although they progressed to the knockout stages for the second successive tournament, this time round they did not emerge from the pool stages undefeated.

England unveiled their 12-man squad for the Commonwealth Games two weeks ahead of the tournament. Four of the players included – John Brake, Dan Norton, Tom Powell and James Rodwell – had been part of the squad in India four years earlier, while eight members of the squad had taken part in the final event of the recent HSBC Sevens World Series, the Marriott London Sevens at Twickenham in May.

The job of leading the team was handed to Tom Mitchell, the leading points scorer in the 2013–14 HSBC Sevens World Series and a nominee for the IRB Sevens Player of the Year, while former Wasps centre Charlie Hayter and London Scottish captain Mark Bright were both called up after impressive performances in the FIRA-AER European Grand Prix Series.

As the two-day event in Glasgow drew near, head coach Simon Amor spoke of how his squad was looking for forward to the challenges that awaited them in Scotland.

"The squad selected has a very good balance of speed, playmaking ability, physicality and the all-important X-factor," he said. "With players returning from long-term injuries, the competition for places has been particularly strong. This has raised the performances in training and the attitude throughout the team has been excellent. We will be looking to bring the experiences and

Left: **James Rodwell breaks a tackle on the way to one of his two tries in the 40–0 group game defeat of Uganda at Ibrox Park, Glasgow, in the 2014 Commonwealth Games Rugby Sevens.**

progress made throughout the Sevens World Series to Glasgow.

"Being part of the bigger team that is Team England at the Commonwealth Games is a unique experience and a very different environment from the one the players are used to on the world circuit. You feed off other sports' successes, see other athletes there and the sheer scale of the village and the competition make it a wonderful occasion."

Amor's side began the competition against Sri Lanka. Four years earlier, they had despatched the Brave Elephants 59–7 in the group stage, and it was a familiar story at Ibrox in 2014 as England put in a convincing performance, scoring nine tries in a 57–0 victory. Mitchell led by example, scoring two tries and five conversions, and England were up and running.

Five hours later they were in action again against Uganda. England had beaten the Rugby Cranes 55–0 in Delhi, but their African opponents were more competitive in Glasgow, eventually going down 40–0 to Amor's team, thanks to a brace of tries apiece from Mitchell and Rodwell.

With the initial warm-up matches over, England prepared to face Australia in their final pool fixture for what would be their biggest test of the day. The form book suggested an English triumph after they had finished one place above the Wallabies in the final 2013–14 HSBC Sevens World Series standings, but Australia had a score to settle after suffering defeats to England in the group stages of the Games in Melbourne in 2006 and again in Delhi in 2010, it was to prove third time lucky for the Australians.

England started the brighter of the two sides in Glasgow and they took a first-half lead when Marcus Watson opted for a delicate chip over the onrushing defensive line. His searing pace saw him outstrip the cover, and he was able to collect possession and touch down moments before sliding over the dead ball line. Mitchell slotted the conversion and England had struck first. The Wallabies replied just before half-time when they worked space for Cameron Clark in the right corner and it was a two-point contest (in England's favour) at the break.

The pivotal moment came in the first minute of the second period when Sean McMahon sliced open the England defence and raced towards the line. The flying Norton eventually caught him, but the England man was subsequently sin-binned for slowing down the release of the ball and while the men in white were a man down, the Wallabies pounced, with McMahon bulldozing his way over the line.

England were on the ropes and worse was to follow when Jesse Parahi stretched for Australia's third try. There was not enough time to stage a recovery, and England were beaten 15–7.

Below: **England captain Tom Mitchell makes a break through the Australian defence during the crucial Pool D encounter at Ibrox Stadium in Glasgow.**

RESULTS: DAY ONE

POOL D

England 57　　　　　　Sri Lanka 0

Tries: Burgess (2), Norton (2), Rodwell (2), Mitchell (2), Watson

Cons: Mitchell (6)

POOL D

England 40　　　　　　Uganda 0

Tries: Ellery, Rodwell (2), Mitchell (2), Brake

Cons: Mitchell (3), Lewis-Pratt (2)

POOL D

England 7　　　　　　Australia 15

Try: Watson

Con: Mitchell

Tries: McMahon, Parahi, Clark

The 2014 Commonwealth Games

DAY TWO

After England's opening-day defeat to Australia meant they were Pool D runners-up behind the Wallabies, Simon Amor's side progressed to the knockout stages of the main medal competition on day two of the competition in Glasgow to face Samoa.

There was an overwhelming sense of déjà vu as England prepared for their crucial Commonwealth Games quarter-final match. For the third Games in succession, they would play the powerful Samoans in the last eight of the tournament.

In Melbourne in 2006 the men in white had emerged 17–14 winners over the Pacific Islanders en route to winning the silver medal, while four years later, in Delhi, they beat Samoa 7–5. They had both been intensely close encounters and, as the third instalment loomed, it seemed another tense and titanic clash was on the cards.

The two teams had met three times during the 2013–14 HSBC Sevens World Series. The Samoans had won in the group phase in South Africa in December and again at the same stage in the USA, but when the two sides had crossed swords in the quarter-finals of the Wellington Sevens in February, it was Amor's side who had come out on top.

Left: **Marcus Watson opened the scoring for England in their quarter-final clash against Samoa at Ibrox Park, Glasgow.**

RESULTS: DAY TWO

CUP QUARTER-FINAL

England 14 **Samoa** 15

Tries: Watson, Norton Tries: Lolo, Toloa (2)

Cons: Lewis-Pratt (2)

PLATE SEMI-FINAL

England 15 **Scotland** 12

Tries: Norton, Powell, Lewis-Pratt Tries: Bennett, Jones

Con: Gregor

PLATE FINAL

England 17 **Wales** 15

Tries: Burgess, Bibby, Watson Tries: Williams, Morgan, Harries

Con: Lewis-Pratt

Top right: Christian Lewis-Pratt was one of England's three try scorers in their semi-final victory over Scotland.

The early exchanges in the quarter-final at Ibrox were unsurprisingly fierce, and although it was England who had to withstand early Samoan pressure, they scored first when Marcus Watson's pace took him over from long range. Team England looked set to take a 7–0 lead into the break, but with the match already in first-half injury time, there was a dramatic reversal of fortune.

Samoa successfully kept the ball alive, knowing the next stoppage would signal the interval and worked a try for Samoa Toloa. It would not have been a disaster, but as Toloa scored, James Rodwell was sin-binned for what the referee adjudged to have been a late challenge. The Pacific Islanders had another play of the ball before half time. They created another scoring opportunity for Toloa and, rather than turning around 7–0 in front, England suddenly found themselves 10–7 in arrears.

Lio Lolo then grabbed a third Samoan try shortly after the restart, and although a sublime chip and chase from Dan Norton handed England hope, it was not enough. Amor's team dropped out of the medal competition after a 15–14 defeat.

"It was disappointing how the quarter-final finished," Norton conceded. "We worked hard for that and then having it taken away from you."

England's medal hopes may have been over, but there was still the Plate competition to complete, and after dusting themselves off after the disappointment of the Samoa game, they showed real character in response.

They met hosts Scotland in the semi-final and three early, unconverted tries were enough to force a 15–12 victory, progressing to the Plate final against Wales.

In the absence of injured Tom Mitchell, deputy captain of the side for Day Two, Phil Burgess, proved the hero of the hour in what turned out to be a pulsating clash. The Welsh scored three first-half tries from Lee Williams, Will Harries and Luke Morgan, and England's only reply came from Dan Bibby after a superb solo break. Bibby again came to the fore after the break when he combined with Burgess to send Watson clear, but with time running out, Wales were still ahead.

The match was won courtesy of a turnover by Rodwell deep in the England 22. The forward burst through the Welsh defence before finding John Brake, who in turn span the ball wide for Burgess to crash over for the try that gave his side a dramatic 17–15 victory.

The final was Tom Powell's last appearance for the team and after representing England at two Commonwealth Games and 40 Sevens World Series tournaments, it was a fitting farewell to a player who had been a stalwart of the Sevens side.

"I feel absolutely privileged to have represented my country around the world," he said. "It has been the biggest honour of my life. The guys I have played with have been immense and I love them all to bits. I will be an avid supporter, as I am now, from here."

IN PROFILE:

Tom Mitchell

Charged with captaining the England Sevens side at the start of 2014, the prolific playmaker responded in superb style, scoring a deluge of points for the Red Rose in the HSBC Sevens World Series.

England Rugby

Position: **Fly-half / Centre**

Age: **25**

Height: **1.77m**

Weight: **86kg**

Representative teams: **Oxford University, Great Britain Students, England Sevens**

In the past two years Tom Mitchell has swapped reading history to making it. His academic interest in the subject stems from his studies at Oxford University, but since he swapped higher education for the globe-trotting rigours of the World Series, the England skipper has recorded his own little bit of history.

He did so at the Marriott London Sevens in May, when he accumulated 48 points at Twickenham to take his personal tally for the 2013–14 Series to a remarkable 358. It was a haul that confirmed Mitchell as England's top scorer for the campaign and saw him become the third Englishman in six years – after Ben Gollings and Dan Norton – to achieve the accolade as the Series' most prolific player.

"Once the season was over, it was good to have achieved it, of course, but as captain I am more focused on the side's results. It was an amazing season, given that I was as a relative fresher to the whole thing at the start."

A try scorer in Oxford's 2011 Varsity Match victory over Cambridge, Mitchell's rise began when he marked his World Sevens debut for England at the Wellington Sevens in February 2012 with three tries in his first three games. And his burgeoning reputation was only enhanced when he captained the Great Britain Students side to the Sevens title at the 2012 World Universities Championships in France.

He signed a full-time contract with the RFU in the summer of 2012, but he did not find himself in the ranks for long. The appointment of Simon Amor as England Sevens Head Coach in 2013 saw a period of rapid evolution for England and, ahead of the USA Sevens in Las Vegas in January the following year, Mitchell replaced Tom Powell as captain.

The promotion may have come as a shock, but Mitchell responded with some fine performances and retained the armband for the Commonwealth Games in Glasgow later in the year.

> "As a rugby player, captaining your country at any level is something you dream about."
>
> **Tom Mitchell**

"As a rugby player, captaining your country at any level is something you dream about," he said. "It opened up my perspective. It made me think a lot about my own game and other people's abilities. Fortunately, my form was coming good at the same time, so when you're playing well and you're able to lead by example on that front, I think that the captaincy becomes relatively easy in a lot of respects.

"It's a very special feeling and I've really enjoyed it. We have a couple of other great leaders, so the burden was shared. I didn't have to try and keep the rabble in check or anything; I just enjoyed the responsibility of it."

Opposite: **Tom Mitchell finished the 2013–14 HSBC Sevens World Series as the top scorer with 358 points, but he missed England's Commonwealth Games plate final victory over Wales because of injury on Day One.**

England Saxons line up for the official introductions before their match against the Irish Wolfhounds at Kingsholm, Gloucester.

England Saxons

The last staging post before players graduate to the senior England squad and a potential full Test debut, the Saxons are an integral part of the RFU development programme. They provide an invaluable opportunity to fine tune a new generation of talent as they look to make the step up from club rugby to the rigours of international competition.

Review 2013–14

WOLFHOUNDS EDGE OUT SAXONS

Saxon coach Jon Callard selected a young side to take on the Ireland Wolfhounds at Gloucester for their first fixture of 2014. However, his young charges were to fall short at Kingsholm against an older and more experienced Irish side.

England Rugby

Saxons 8
Wolfhounds 14

Date: **25 January 2014**
Stadium: **Kingsholm,**
       Gloucester
Attendance: **8,000**
Referee: **Ian Davies**
       (Wales)

If the remit of the Saxons is to blood new players, Callard and his coaching staff undoubtedly ticked all the boxes when he announced his starting XV to face the Irish. England's second team was bursting with players new to this level and featured just three full internationals – fly-half Freddie Burns, scrum-half Joe Simpson and wing Charlie Sharples with eight caps between them.

The captaincy was handed to Northampton flanker Calum Clark on his Saxons debut. The Saints back rower was joined by fellow newcomers Anthony Watson, Sam Hill, Alex Waller, Charlie Matthews, Luke Wallace and Dave Ewers, while the inclusion of half-backs Henry Slade and Dave Lewis on the bench took the Exeter Chief's match-day contingent up to four players.

"Calum [Clark] has been a positive influence from the moment he arrived in camp," said Joe Lydon, the Rugby Football Union's head of international player development and the man presiding over the Saxons set-up. "He commands the respect of the group and I'm sure he will lead from the front. Freddie [Burns] has also made an outstanding contribution in the time he's been with us and he will be vice-captain."

A crowd of 8,000 descended on Kingsholm to witness the Anglo-Irish clash, and although

Left: **Fly-half Freddie Burns landed a penalty for the Saxons against the Wolfhounds at Kingsholm**

it was a relatively low-scoring encounter, it was nonetheless an intriguing match in which the home side enjoyed a 60 per cent share of possession but could not translate that dominance into points.

Ireland drew first blood in the fifth minute of the contest when they drove an attacking lineout ball towards the England line. The Red Rose pack successfully halted the momentum, but they could not stop scrum-half Isaac Boss as he darted from the back of the maul for the opening try. Ian Madigan converted to take Ireland into a 7–0 lead.

Twenty minutes would pass before Callard's side found a response. Wolfhounds wing Darren Cave spilled possession and Bath flyer Anthony Watson was gratefully on hand to scoop up the loose ball, ignite the afterburners and sprint a full 50 metres for the try. Burns' attempted conversion slammed against the post and England trailed 7–5.

The Saxons were then made to pay for a momentary lapse in concentration on the half hour when Madigan took a quick tap penalty and was allowed to squeeze over the try line from close range. After the Leinster fly-half's conversion sailed over, England headed to the dressing room 14–5 behind.

The Saxons had a strong wind behind their backs in the second half, and although it helped them edge the territorial battle, the points would not come. Burns hit the upright with a penalty attempt once again before he managed to land another three-pointer on the hour mark to cut his side's deficit to only six points.

The Red Rose probed the Irish defence consistently in the final quarter and full-back Elliot Daly went desperately close in the 75th minute but was ultimately held up short. There was still time for two further near-misses from Daly and then Burns, but the Wolfhounds clung on desperately to record a hard-fought 14–8 victory.

The result may have been disappointing, but after the match Callard preferred to focus on the team's performance and the number of his players who he believed had taken a significant step closer to breaking into Stuart Lancaster's senior squad.

"I think potentially out of this group there are numerous options to go forward into the full squad," he said. "Whether that will happen next week, across the course of the 6 Nations or the summer tour, I can't say, but I think if you come back in two to three years' time, this could be a really good marking-point for English rugby. We were very aggressive with selection in terms of pushing young players."

> "We put down a marker tonight for English rugby with the number of youngsters we picked, and the future is exciting."
>
> **Jon Callard**

England Saxons 8	Irish Wolfhounds 14
15 Elliot DALY	15 Felix JONES
14 Anthony WATSON	14 Fergus MCFADDEN
13 → Matt HOPPER	13 → Robbie HENSHAW
12 → Sam HILL	12 Darren CAVE
11 Charlie SHARPLES	11 → Craig GILROY
10 Freddie BURNS	10 Ian MADIGAN
9 → Joe SIMPSON	9 → Isaac BOSS
1 → Alex WALLER	1 → David KILCOYNE
2 → Jamie GEORGE	2 → Rob HERRING
3 → Tom MERCEY	3 → Martin MOORE
4 → Charlie MATTHEWS	4 Iain HENDERSON
5 George KRUIS	5 Dan TUOHY
6 Callum CLARK (c)	6 Rhys RUDDOCK (c)
7 Luke WALLACE	7 Tommy O'DONNELL
8 → Dave EWERS	8 Robin COPELAND

REPLACEMENTS	REPLACEMENTS
2 ← 16 Dave WARD	2 ← 16 Richardt STRAUSS
1 ← 17 Nathan CATT	1 ← 17 Jack MCGRATH
3 ← 18 Scott WILSON	3 ← 18 Stephen ARCHER
4 ← 19 Elliott STOOKE	19 Robbie DIACK
8 ← 20 Sam DICKINSON	20 Jordi MURPHY
9 ← 21 Dave LEWIS	21 Kieron MARMION
12 ← 22 Henry SLADE	13 ← 22 Ian KEATLEY
13 ← 23 Rob MILLER	11 ← 23 Simon ZEBO

SCORES	SCORES
Try: **Watson**	Tries: **Boss, Madigan**
	Cons: **Madigan (2)**
Pen: **Burns**	

Review 2013–14

SAXONS STALEMATE IN SCOTSTOUN

England had just seven days to recuperate from their narrow defeat to the Wolfhounds before they took on Scotland A in Glasgow. The Saxons had lost their last two meetings against the Auld Enemy and were desperate to avoid a third successive defeat when the two sides met at the Scotstoun Stadium in February.

England
Rugby

Scotland A 16

Saxons 16

Date: **31 January 2014**
Stadium: **Scotstoun,
Glasgow**
Attendance: **3,004**
Referee: **Laurent
Cardona (France)**

The Saxons are a team designed to bridge the gap between club and Test rugby. The majority of its players are yet to experience the red hot atmosphere of a senior international, but there have been occasions when capped players have returned to the Saxons set-up. It is extremely rare, however, for a player who has already made his full England Test debut to then represent the Saxons for the first time.

Bath's Kyle Eastmond did just that against the Scots, when he was named at centre for the Glasgow game. The versatile rugby league convert had played in both Tests during England's tour to Argentina the previous summer and, eight months later, he was poised to make his bow for the Saxons.

The inclusion of Eastmond was one of four changes to the back line, with Bath flyer Semesa Rokoduguni, Leicester wing Adam Thompstone and Gloucester scrum-half Dan Robson all called up. There were also four new faces in the pack, with Saxons debuts handed to Harlequins hooker Dave Ward, Newcastle prop Scott Wilson, Gloucester lock Elliott Stooke and Northampton flanker Sam Dickinson.

"This group of young players worked hard in both preparing for and playing against an experienced Wolfhounds side at Kingsholm," said the RFU's Joe Lydon. "We didn't deliver the win on Saturday, but created some good opportunities, and the team are building their knowledge of what is expected and our knowledge of them as a squad is also increasing.

"We are under no illusion how tough it will be for us in Glasgow against Scotland

A, who've done well against us at this level in recent years, but our players have a lot of talent, endeavour and a willingness to work for each other to build on their club form.

"Our aim is to continue working with them in an evolving, long-term programme that compliments the excellent work done at their clubs in developing players capable of achieving success at club and at senior international level at the World Cups in 2015, 2019 and beyond."

England began the match with real intensity, and Freddie Burns was on target with a third-minute penalty, only for Scotland scrum-half Henry Pyrgos to reply two minutes later with a drop goal. Robson was sent to the sin bin in the 17th minute and while he was cooling his heels in the dugout, Pyrgos landed a penalty to give the Scots a slender lead.

Above: **England Saxons lock Elliot Stooke gathers a lineout in the 16–16 draw at Scotstoun.**

Opposite: **Scotland A centre Alex Grove (left) needs the help of Rob Harley to stop England Saxons replacement fly-half Henry Slade.**

"We knew it was going to be a tough game. They always are with that great rivalry when we face a Scotland team."

Joe Lydon

The England scrum was proving a potent weapon as the game unfolded, and when two scrums in quick succession collapsed with the Saxons on the front foot and the Scottish line within range, French referee Laurent Cardona decided he had no option but to award a penalty try. Burns converted, and the visitors were 10–6 to the good at the break.

The Saxons fly-half added a penalty soon after the restart, but was then forced to hobble off with an injury. His replacement, Exeter's Henry Slade, had only been on the pitch for four minutes before he was shown yellow for a professional foul.

Scotland did not squander their numerical superiority, and moments after Slade's dismissal, they worked enough space for wing Byron McGuigan to touch down in the left corner. Substitute fly-half Tom Heathcote made no mistake with the conversion, and the match was locked at 10–10 with 20 minutes remaining.

England edged back in front with an Elliot Daly penalty after the Scots had been penalized for an illegal turnover at the breakdown and, as the clock wound down, the Saxons seemed to be on course for victory, only for Heathcote to step forward with two minutes remaining to land a penalty after Luke Wallace was adjudged to have impeded a Scottish player off the ball.

The match finished 16–16 and although the Saxons had ended their losing sequence against the Scots, the result did not spark wild celebrations in the England camp.

"I'm as disappointed as the players are not to have got a win, but they have learned a lot about how to play international football," Lydon said after the match. "To lose two players was crucial. Little bits of ill-discipline at key moments in the game that could have cost us a lot more."

Scotland A 16		England Saxons 16	
15	Jack CUTHBERT	15	Rob MILLER
14	Dougie FIFE	14 →	Samesa ROKODUGUNI
13	Mark BENNETT	13	Elliot DALY
12	Alex GROVE	12	Kyle EASTMOND
11 →	Bryon MCGUIGAN	11	Adam THOMPSTONE
10 →	Greig TONKS	10 →	Freddie BURNS
9 →	Henry PYRGOS	9 →	Dan ROBSON
1 →	Gordon REID	1 →	Alex WALLER
2 →	Fraser BROWN	2 →	Dave WARD
3 →	Jon WELSH	3 →	Scott WILSON
4 →	Kieran LOW	4 →	Elliot STOOKE
5	Jonny GRAY (c)	5	George KRUIS
6	Rob HARLEY	6	Calum CLARK (c)
7 →	Blair COWAN	7	Luke WALLACE
8	Ally HOGG	8 →	Sam DICKINSON

REPLACEMENTS		REPLACEMENTS	
2 ←	16 Kevin BRYCE	2 ←	16 Jamie GEORGE
1 ←	17 Alex ALLAN	1 ←	17 Nathan CATT
3 ←	18 Ed KALMAN	3 ←	18 Kieran BROOKES
4 ←	19 Olly ATKINS	4 ←	19 Charlie MATTHEWS
7 ←	20 Tyrone HOLMES	8 ←	20 Dave EWERS
9 ←	21 Grayson HART	9 ←	21 Joe SIMPSON
10 ←	22 Tom HEATHCOTE	10 ←	22 Henry SLADE
11 ←	23 Richie VERNON	14 ←	23 Charlie SHARPLES

SCORES

Try: McGuigan
Con: Heathcote
Pens: Pyrgos, Heathcote
Drop: Pyrgos

SCORES

Try: Penalty try
Con: Burns
Pens: Burns (2), Daly

The Webb Ellis Trophy will be lifted at Twickenham on 31 October 2015.

The Rugby World Cup Trophy Tour

After visiting Japan, Australia, Fiji, Madagascar, Argentina, Uruguay, USA, the UAE and China in 2014, the Webb Ellis Trophy will be on tour in the UK in 2015 between 10 June and 18 September. For more details visit **www.rugbyworldcup.com.**

Rugby World Cup 2015 Preview

With an estimated three million supporters attending 48 matches and a global television audience to reach more than four billion, the eighth instalment of the Rugby World Cup in England in 2015 will be the greatest rugby tournament in the sport's history.

England
Rugby

Twickenham Prepares to Welcome the World

THE RUGBY WORLD CUP COUNTDOWN BEGINS

With HQ set to host ten games during Rugby World Cup 2015, including both semi-finals and the final, Twickenham will be the centre of global attention in 2015 as the best teams on the planet descend on England to compete for the coveted Webb Ellis Trophy.

Twickenham has come a long way since it hosted its first international match more than a century ago. In front of a capacity crowd of 18,000, which numbered King George V among its ranks, the inaugural Test in 1910 saw the Red Rose despatch Wales 11–6. HQ has been the spiritual home of English rugby ever since.

The famous old stadium has undergone countless modifications and radical redevelopment in the intervening years, but as the ground prepares to act as the centrepiece of the Rugby World Cup for a second time, it has lost none of its unique atmosphere or sense of history.

A total of 13 stadiums will stage games during the 2015 tournament, but for Stuart Lancaster's England side, HQ will be home. Three of their four Pool A fixtures, including the tournament opener against Fiji on 18 September, are being played in southwest London and should they progress safely to the knockout stages, all their subsequent matches will unfold in the familiar surroundings of Twickenham. Home advantage will be a crucial part of England's armoury, and Lancaster is convinced the support generated within the stadium can propel his side deep into the latter stages of the tournament.

"The best games at Twickenham have been influenced without a doubt by the fans," he said. "The fans create an unbelievable energy and English support at its best is better than anyone's in the world. They help the team, they carry the team and the players feel it

massively. The fans feel they are supporting a team that is young and ambitious, that wants to have a go, and the players respond likewise. It is a virtuous circle.

"To win top games, ultimately you need motivation, to feel why playing for this team is special. The motivation is not a little part of the jigsaw. It's a big, big part of the jigsaw. It is the difference sometimes between winning and losing. The feeling inside the changing room at Twickenham is incredibly powerful. Look at the history and heritage that is on the walls. As a player sat here

Above: **Thousands of supporters will cheer on England during the Rugby World Cup 2015.**

you know it is a unique place to be. It is an unbelievable feeling."

Rugby World Cup rugby first came to the ground in 1991, when the Red Rose faced the All Blacks in the competition's opening match. Three more matches, including the final (an agonizing loss to Australia for Geoff Cooke's team), were staged at the stadium that year, and while England was not the principal host of the 1999 tournament, Twickenham was the setting for six more games. Overall, the Red Rose have won five of their eight World Cup games at the ground, scoring 35 tries and 320 points.

A capacity crowd of 56,208 crammed into HQ to watch the 1991 final between England and the Wallabies. The stadium can now hold over 82,000 and demand for tickets in 2015 has been phenomenal, with an incredible 650,000 applications for the pool game between the Red Rose and the Wallabies in September and 500,000 requests for tickets for the final the following month.

We are thrilled with demand for tickets a year out from the tournament," said Debbie Jevans, the England Rugby 2015 chief executive. "The record level of demand we have seen is a terrific indicator of the general interest and excitement for the Rugby World Cup."

Staging a Test at Twickenham is a huge logistical feat. A small army of 1,000 gatemen and stewards have to be deployed at the stadium's various entrances, and turnstiles and pre-match checks have to be carried out before Richmond Council issues a safety certificate for the match.

An estimated 2,500 chefs and support staff in 30 separate kitchens have to be charged with preparing in excess of 10,000 match-day meals, while thirsty supporters will get through an average of 90,000 pints during the day's proceedings.

The logistics do not end with the sound of the final whistle. The RFU has to ensure the 82,000-plus fans make their way home safely. Some 35,000 will head to Twickenham mainline station, while around 6,000 are expected to take the shuttle bus service from the stadium to Richmond tube station. Twickenham station is currently undergoing a £5 million refurbishment ahead of the tournament.

"The station will be improved in time for the Rugby World Cup and will help create a better first impression for fans as they make their way to the station," said Network Rail's commercial director Sam McCarthy. "There will also be longer-term benefits for

Below: **Twickenham first hosted the Rugby World Cup final in 1991 when England faced Australia.**

passengers and commuters who use the station every day and those who will attend future sporting events at Twickenham."

The Rugby World Cup 2015 will bring other new challenges, as England's pool games against Fiji, Wales and Australia all kick off at eight in the evening. The decision to stage the matches at night prompted the RFU to review the stadium's floodlighting, and when fans arrive for the late games in 2015, HQ will be bathed in brand-new LED lighting.

"We were one of the first stadiums in Europe to install mid-tier LEDs and believe we are now the first to have LED floodlights designed," said Richard Knight, the stadium director at Twickenham. "Better-quality lighting will allow us to improve the viewing experience for fans both in the stadium and at home, by keeping ahead of fast-moving developments in TV technology. This innovative product also has the added benefit of being more energy efficient and requires less maintenance."

New structures will also be popping up around the stadium to cater for the flood of supporters making their way to the ground for the ten matches. The size of one-and-a-half pitches, the biggest will be the "Twickenham Pavilion" in the North Car Park which will have the capacity to cater for up to 3,000 people.

Some of the planned work ahead of the World Cup has already been completed, and in late 2013 the stadium's famous World Rugby Museum, which features over 25,000 exhibits, including the only surviving shirt from the very first Test in 1871 between

"The best games at Twickenham have been influenced without a doubt by the fans. English support at its best is better than anyone's in the world. They help the team, they carry the team and the players feel it massively."

Stuart Lancaster

Left: **The Rugby World Cup 1991 also saw Twickenham stage six matches, including the two semi-finals.**

England and Scotland, was officially reopened after a major revamp.

"It's great that we now have a museum fit to welcome the rugby world when it arrives in England in 2015 for the World Cup," said curator Michael Rowe. "The World Rugby Museum gives a unique insight into rugby. It's a great way for people to learn about the history of the game, from its origins in Rugby School to the present day, regardless of which team or nation they support."

From a playing perspective, Twickenham's preparations for the Rugby World Cup will include two warm-up games for Lancaster's team, with France visiting HQ in August and Ireland arriving in London the following month.

World Rugby announced that England had won the race to host the Rugby World Cup in July 2009, beating off competition from South Africa and Italy. "We have been trusted with making a great competition and providing a great spectacle," said the then RFU chairman Martyn Thomas after the announcement. "Australia did an immense job [in 2003], France raised the bar [in 2007] and we have got to raise it again."

Preparations for the tournament began in earnest the day after World Rugby's decision, and with the prolonged countdown to kick-off now almost over, Twickenham is poised to play host to the biggest World Cup party ever.

Preparations to host Rugby World Cup 2015 began in earnest with England Rugby 2015 brought on board to deliver the tournament. Since its inception the organising committee has unveiled host cities and venues across England and Cardiff, launched ticket sales resulting in record demand during the September general sale, announced Team Bases, created the World Largest Scrum (made up of 1,008 participants) and hosted volunteer recruitment events across the country. With under one year to go until the tournament, and major announcements set for early 2015, the countdown is on for what is set to be the greatest Rugby World Cup ever.

Right: Martin Johnson made three Twickenham appearances at the Rugby World Cup 1999 before lifting the trophy four years later.

England Rugby

England at the Rugby World Cup

TOURNAMENT RECORD SINCE 1987

One of the greatest global gatherings in sport, the Rugby World Cup has seen England proudly fly the flag for European rugby. They remain the only nation from the northern hemisphere to have lifted the Webb Ellis Cup after their famous victory over the Wallabies in Sydney in 2003. The Red Rose are also the only Home Union side to have qualified for the knockout stages at all seven tournaments to date, and are one of only two countries (along with Australia) to have reached successive finals.

Jointly staged by Australia and New Zealand, the inaugural World Cup in 1987 was a journey into the unknown for the Red Rose, and it proved to be a chastening experience for an England side, captained by Wakefield wing Mike Harrison, which had collected the Wooden Spoon in the 6 Nations earlier in the year.

Their tournament began against the Wallabies in Sydney, but there was to be no dream start to the new World Cup era for England as the hosts emerged 19–6 winners. Although England went on to record

comfortable victories over Japan and the USA to finish as pool runners-up, there was no great optimism emanating from the camp as they prepared to face Wales in the quarter-finals.

The Anglo-Welsh battle in Brisbane that ensued was desperately disappointing from an English perspective. Wales scored three tries to none in their 16–3 triumph and England headed home to reflect forlornly on the vagaries of this new global tournament.

It was an altogether different, more uplifting story in 1991 when England agreed to stage

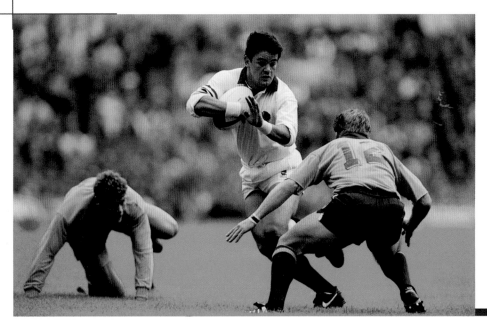

Left: Will Carling captained England at the 1991 Rugby World Cup on home soil.

Above: **Jonny Wilkinson's drop goals sealed World Cup glory in Sydney in 2003.**

Above right: **New Zealand wing Jonah Lomu ended England's challenge at Cape Town in 1995.**

the competition and with the country gripped by World Cup fever, the team responded superbly on the pitch and went all the way to the final at HQ.

An 18–12 defeat to the All Blacks at Twickenham in the tournament opener failed to dampen the national sense of anticipation and after winning the remainder of their pool games, France and then Scotland were dismissed in the knockout stages to take the Red Rose to the final against Australia.

In a low-scoring clash at Twickenham, it was a prop of all players – the Wallabies' Tony Daly – who scored the only try of the match from short range. The redoubtable boot of full-back Jonathan Webb was responsible for all of England's points in a heart-breaking 12–6 defeat, but the indelible memory many England fans left Twickenham with was David Campese's controversial knock-on from Peter Winterbottom's attempted pass to Rory Underwood. Had the ball found him, the try line was at Underwood's mercy, but to the vocal disbelief of the England faithful, referee Derek Bevan declined to award the penalty try.

The reintegration of South Africa into the world of sport following the end of Apartheid saw the World Cup head to the Rainbow Nation in 1995, and it was plain sailing for Jack Rowell's side in the group stages as they recorded victories over Western Samoa, Italy and Argentina.

A dramatic, glorious, Rob Andrew drop-goal from the 10-metre line in injury-time in the quarter-final against the Wallabies

at Newlands took England through to the last four, but then they ran into a muscular wrecking ball by the name of Jonah Lomu in the semi-final, and his unforgettable four-try blitz for the All Blacks in Cape Town destroyed England's challenge.

The 1999 World Cup, the first of the professional era, staged across Europe, was the first experience of the game's greatest stage for Messrs Woodward, Wilkinson and Johnson, and although rugby immortality lay in wait for all three, this did not prove to be a tournament at which England excelled.

A defeat to New Zealand in the pool phase condemned England to play in the (now defunct) quarter-final play-offs, and although Fiji were comfortably swept aside at Twickenham, courtesy of tries from Neil Back, Nick Beal, Phil Greening and Dan Luger, victory merely postponed the side's exit from the tournament.

Defending champions South Africa were their opponents in the quarter-finals at the Stade de France, and England were bemused bystanders as fly-half Jannie de Beer knocked over a world record five drop-goals – and 34 points in total – as the Springboks ran out 44–21 winners.

World Cup rugby returned to Australia in 2003 and, in stark contrast to their visit Down Under in 1987, England found the Antipodean atmosphere rather to their liking as they finally ended the southern hemisphere's monopoly of the competition and came home triumphantly with the silverware.

It was the first tournament to feature five-team groups, and Clive Woodward's 6 Nations champions amassed a staggering 255 points as they swept aside South Africa, Samoa, Uruguay and Georgia in Pool C to progress serenely to the business end of the competition.

Wales were despatched 28–17 in the quarter-final in Brisbane, 16 years after the result had gone the other way, thanks to 23 points from Jonny Wilkinson's boot, and the fly-half was just as unerringly accurate in the semi-final against France at the Telstra Stadium, kicking five penalties and three trademark drop-goals to seal an emphatic 24–7 win.

The final against the Wallabies, the reigning champions, was as nerve shredding as it was ultimately euphoric for England. In any other match the sight of Jason Robinson scampering over the line for England's try would have endured as the iconic image of the contest, but it was Wilkinson who stole the headlines – and the Webb Ellis Cup from the Australians – in injury time in Sydney.

His famous drop-goal would have been magnificent had it been delivered by his legendary left foot. That it came off his right boot was almost unbelievable in the context of the match, and as it sailed safely between the uprights, one Australian commentator reluctantly observed "that surely is the stairway to rugby heaven for England". So it proved, and England were the world champions.

The mantle of World Cup winners did not seem to sit comfortably with Brian Ashton's England squad as they staged their defence of the title four years later in France, and pre-tournament suspicions that the Red Rose would struggle in 2007 were confirmed when the Springboks thumped them 36–0 in Paris in their second group-stage match.

Initial impressions can be deceptive, however. England made no mistake in their other Pool A clashes, against Tonga, Samoa and the USA, and in a reunion of the protagonists from the 2003 final, the Red Rose edged out the Wallabies 12–10 in the quarter-final in Marseille, thanks to four more Wilkinson penalties.

Two drop-goals, two penalties and a Josh Lewsey try were enough to fend off the French in the semi-final and, against the odds, England found themselves in the final,

> ## "I can't say enough about the team, because we had the lead and we lost it, but we came back. And I can't say enough about Wilko at the end."
>
> ## Martin Johnson after the 2003 World Cup final

in which they would again face their cruel tormentors from the group stage, South Africa.

England's transformation from their Parisian mauling five weeks earlier was remarkable, but for a rare time in his Test career, Wilkinson emerged second best in a battle of the kickers.

There were no tries at the Stade de France and although Wilkinson made no mistake with the two penalty chances that came his way, Percy Montgomery was on target with all four of his three-point opportunities, with Francois Steyn adding a fifth, and a 15–6 Springbok victory ended England's reign as champions.

The 2011 World Cup in New Zealand saw Martin Johnson's famous scowl on the touchline rather than in the engine room of the pack, but the World Cup-winning captain's famous motivational abilities failed to lift his team, and England struggled.

It all began smoothly enough with narrow wins over Scotland and Argentina and more comfortable victories over Georgia and Romania in Pool B, but as England's tournament began to unravel in the wake of some antics off the pitch, their performance on the pitch suffered.

They went out in the quarter-finals to France in Auckland and paid a heavy price for a dismal first-half performance in which they leaked 16 unanswered points. Tries from Ben Foden and Mark Cueto after the restart restored a degree of respectability, but it was too little too late, and England headed home on the back of a 19–12 defeat.

England's faltering displays in New Zealand prompted Martin Johnson to resign as team manager and ushered in the Stuart Lancaster era. He will become the seventh coach to attempt to lead the Red Rose to World Cup glory when the tournament returns to England in 2015.

Opposite: **England captain Martin Johnson lifed the iconic Webb Ellis Cup in Australia in 2003.**

1987

England 6	Australia 19	SYDNEY	23 MAY 1987	Pool
England 60	Japan 7	SYDNEY	30 MAY 1987	Pool
England 34	USA 6	SYDNEY	3 JUNE 1987	Pool
England 3	Wales 16	BRISBANE	8 JUNE 1987	QF

1991

England 12	New Zealand 18	TWICKENHAM	3 OCT 1991	Pool
England 36	Italy 6	TWICKENHAM	8 OCT 1991	Pool
England 37	USA 9	TWICKENHAM	11 OCT 1991	Pool
England 19	France 10	PARC DES PRINCES	19 OCT 1991	QF
England 9	Scotland 6	MURRAYFIELD	26 OCT 1991	SF
England 6	Australia 12	TWICKENHAM	2 NOV 1991	FINAL

1995

England 24	Argentina 18	DURBAN	27 MAY 1995	Pool
England 27	Italy 20	DURBAN	31 MAY 1995	Pool
England 44	Samoa 22	DURBAN	4 JUNE 1995	Pool
England 25	Australia 22	CAPE TOWN	11 JUNE 1995	QF
England 29	New Zealand 45	CAPE TOWN	18 JUNE 1995	SF

1999

England 67	Italy 7	TWICKENHAM	2 OCT 1999	Pool
England 16	New Zealand 30	TWICKENHAM	9 OCT 1999	Pool
England 101	Tonga 10	TWICKENHAM	15 OCT 1999	Pool
England 45	Fiji 24	TWICKENHAM	20 OCT 1999	Playoff
England 21	South Africa 44	STADE DE FRANCE	24 OCT 1999	QF

2003

England 84	Georgia 6	PERTH	12 OCT 2003	Pool
England 25	South Africa 6	PERTH	18 OCT 2003	Pool
England 35	Samoa 22	MELBOURNE	26 OCT 2003	Pool
England 111	Uruguay 13	BRISBANE	2 NOV 2003	Pool
England 28	Wales 17	BRISBANE	9 NOV 2003	QF
England 24	France 7	SYDNEY	16 NOV 2003	SF
England 20	Australia 17	SYDNEY	22 NOV 2003	FINAL

2007

England 28	USA 10	LENS	8 SEP 2007	Pool
England 0	South Africa 36	STADE DE FRANCE	14 SEP 2007	Pool
England 44	Samoa 22	NANTES	22 SEP 2007	Pool
England 36	Tonga 20	PARC DES PRINCES	28 SEP 2007	Pool
England 12	Australia 10	MARSEILLE	6 OCT 2007	QF
England 14	France 9	STADE DE FRANCE	13 OCT 2007	SF
England 6	South Africa 15	STADE DE FRANCE	20 OCT 2007	FINAL

2011

England 13	Argentina 9	DUNEDIN	10 SEP 2011	Pool
England 41	Georgia 10	DUNEDIN	18 SEP 2011	Pool
England 67	Romania 3	DUNEDIN	24 SEP 2011	Pool
England 16	Scotland 12	AUCKLAND	1 OCT 2011	Pool
England 12	France 19	AUCKLAND	8 OCT 2011	QF

LEADING POINTS-SCORERS AT THE WORLD CUP: TOP TEN

1	277	Jonny **WILKINSON**	(1999–2011)
2	99	Jonathan **WEBB**	(1987–1991)
3	85	Rob **ANDREW**	(1987–1995)
4	84	Paul **GRAYSON**	(1999–2003)
5	49	Rory **UNDERWOOD**	(1987–1995)
6	35	Will **GREENWOOD**	(1999–2003)
7	30	Chris **ASHTON**	(2011)
=	30	Josh **LEWSEY**	(2003–2007)
=	30	Dan **LUGER**	(1999–2003)
10	25	Neil **BACK**	(1995–2003)
=	25	Jason **ROBINSON**	(2003–2007)

Wing Marland Yarde made a big impression on England's summer tour of New Zealand.

The Players

By any measure of success, 2014 was a year in which England sides excelled on the international stage. Three major trophies were placed proudly in the trophy cabinet at Twickenham in just six months and England's teams prospered at all levels of the game.

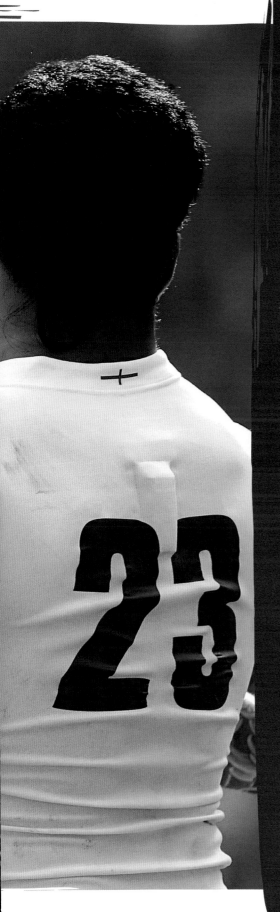

England Men: Players of the Year

Rugby remains first and foremost a team game, but individuals will inevitably shine brightly over the course of a season, and there was certainly no shortage of standout individual performers for Stuart Lancaster's side in 2014 as they claimed the Triple Crown before crossing swords with the All Blacks in the summer.

Reputations were enhanced from the front row through to full-back, and it was a young England team brimming with attacking intent. The head coach handed debuts to six players during the RBS 6 Nations and the summer tour, and while the likes of Luther Burrell and Jack Nowell flew the flag admirably for the international new boys, the older heads in the squad, such as Danny Care and Mike Brown, were far from eclipsed.

Jack Nowell is congratulated by Manu Tuilagi (23) after scoring England's third try during the RBS 6 Nations Championship match against Italy in Rome.

IN PROFILE:

Danny Care

A veteran of 50 Tests for England, the Harlequins No.9 was in mesmeric form the men in white during the RBS 6 Nations.

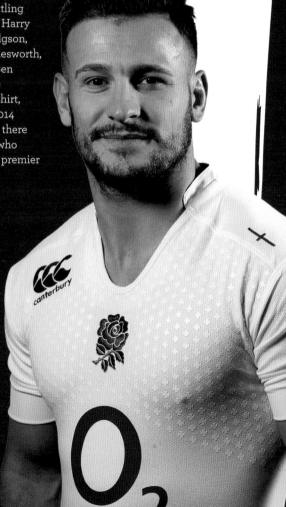

England Rugby

Position: **Scrum-half**
Age: **27**
Height: **1.77m**
Weight: **87kg**
Caps: **50**

In comparison to many in the current England set-up, Danny Care has emerged as something of an elder statesman in the ranks. The Harlequins scrum-half is now the second most-capped player in Stuart Lancaster's squad, behind Dylan Hartley, and while most of his team-mates began their Test careers in the aftermath of England's exit from the 2011 World Cup in New Zealand, Care has been ploughing his international furrow since 2008.

The No.9 is far from his dotage, however, and his instinctive and incisive performances throughout the RBS 6 Nations in 2014 were arguably the best of his career. Care has always played the game at a frenetic pace, and he demonstrated he clearly has no intention of slowing down during the 2014 championship.

Selected ahead of Lee Dickson for the opener against France in Paris, he began the tournament with a bang. His impudent, short-range drop-goal in the second half was typical of him, while it was his quick tap and jinking dart that sliced open the French defence to pave the way for Mike Brown's try.

Another, longer-range drop-goal against Scotland at Murrayfield followed a week later, while it was his exquisite flat pass for Luther Burrell's opening try in Edinburgh that underlined the scrum-half's attacking impact.

Care scored the first try of his international career against the All Blacks in Christchurch in the summer of 2008, and his sixth Test score came in spectacular style during England's victory over Ireland at Twickenham in February, when he raced on to Brown's inviting pass before outpacing the cover to touch down under the posts. He repeated the

trick against Wales at HQ six days later with another quickly taken tap penalty in only the fifth minute that left a static Welsh defence flat footed, embarrassed and powerless to stop him from diving triumphantly over the line.

Care has consistently had to earn his place in the side, battling variously with Harry Ellis, Paul Hodgson, Richard Wigglesworth, Dickson and Ben Youngs for the coveted No.9 shirt, but after the 2014 championship there was no doubt who was England's premier scrum-half.

IN PROFILE:

Courtney Lawes

A Premiership winner for Northampton, the rampaging Saints second row came of age in England colours during the 2014 campaign.

England Rugby

Position: **Second row/ back row**
Age: **25**
Height: **2.00m**
Weight: **111kg**
Caps: **36**

A phenomenal natural athlete, a dangerous ball carrier and arguably the most destructive tackler in the squad, Courtney Lawes has caught the eye on England duty ever since he made his debut from the bench against the Wallabies in 2009. The six-foot-seven-inch Northampton lock is a player who is difficult to ignore, whatever the match scenario.

However, the big hits and the rampaging runs have often belied his technical ability. Lawes may look like a three-quarter out wide with the ball in hand, but he is first and foremost a fine lineout exponent and a powerful scrummager, and he truly came of age in the England engine room during the RBS 6 Nations.

The Red Rose began the tournament robbed of the services of Geoff Parling after shoulder surgery and, for the first time in his international career, Lawes was the senior partner in the second row, charged with the responsibility of running the England lineout.

Statistics can sometimes be misleading, but in this case they speak volumes. England had 67 lineouts on their own throw during the course of the championship and only six went astray. They were a perfect eight from eight against Paul O'Connell's Ireland and safely secured possession 22 times from the throw against Scotland.

The tournament was a personal triumph for Lawes, who celebrated his 25th birthday the day after England's victory over Ireland at Twickenham, but his trademark dynamism across the park was not diminished by his added responsibility, and he was also in incredible form on the summer tour of New Zealand.

The third Test in Hamilton in particular was Lawes at his very best, and no one in the England side completed more turnovers or won more lineout ball than the Saints star, while his tackle count was second only to Chris Robshaw and Tom Wood.

Lawes may have been blessed with all the natural attributes to become a high-class Test player, but 2014 was the year in which his intelligence and maturity truly emerged from the shadow of his physical prowess.

IN PROFILE:

Mike Brown

In a season in which the full-back could do no wrong, Brown was England's top try scorer in the Championship in 2014.

England Rugby

Position: **Full-back/wing**
Age: **29**
Height: **1.83m**
Weight: **92kg**
Caps: **33**

Mike Brown's first 21 appearances for England were undoubtedly impressive. The Harlequins full-back was a model of courageous consistency under the high ball, his defence was robust and his ability to break the first tackle made him a dangerous counter-attacker.

In the 2014 RBS 6 Nations, however, he raised his game to a new, rarefied level, and by the end of the tournament it had become impossible to refute the case for Brown's status as the best full-back in world rugby.

He began the championship in irresistible form. His try against the French in Paris showcased his deceptive power as he burst his way through a tangle of defenders in the left corner; his second-half score in the 20–0 victory over Scotland in Edinburgh was all about support play; and his predatory eye for the line against the Italians in Rome highlighted the full-back's searing pace.

Four tries in five games in part explains his richly deserved accolade of Player of the Tournament, but the scores were only the tip of the iceberg. His overall performance in the championship was nothing short of sensational. No England player beat more defenders (25) or made more clean breaks (10) than Brown. His 534 metres gained was the most from any of Stuart Lancaster's players, and his total of 64 carries was the highest in the squad.

His unbelievable form continued on the summer tour to New Zealand, starting in all three Tests against the All Blacks, and once again his try in the second game in Dunedin only told half the story: his overall contribution against the No.1 side in the world was immense.

Brown may have been overlooked for the 2011 World Cup in New Zealand, but England fans will be hoping for his Midas touch again when the latest instalment of the tournament kicks off in 2015.

IN PROFILE:

Owen Farrell

The young playmaker with the golden boot, Farrell is already sixth on the list of all-time points scorers for England.

England Rugby

Position: **Fly-half/ centre**

Age: **23**

Height: **1.88m**

Weight: **96kg**

Caps: **30**

It was never going to be easy following in the footsteps of Jonny Wilkinson. The retired England fly-half was as iconic on the world stage as he was prolific on the pitch, and following his Test swansong at the 2011 World Cup in New Zealand, many feared for whoever was handed the No.10 shirt.

Owen Farrell inherited it ahead of the 2012 RBS 6 Nations, but it was in 2014 that the Saracens fly-half truly emerged from the shadow of his illustrious predecessor.

Farrell was as accurate as ever with the boot throughout the year. The youngster's ability to dissect the uprights consistently is more than a little reminiscent of the man he succeeded in the side, but it was his game management, his vision and his growing threat with ball in hand that saw Farrell arrive as a fully-fledged Test fly-half.

There was no better illustration of his arrival than in England's game against Italy in Rome in the final round of the 2014 RBS 6 Nations. Farrell's eight successful kicks from eight attempts underlined his metronomic brilliance from the tee, but it was his try – the second of his international career – that highlighted the way in which his view of the game had changed: he danced through the *Azzurri* defence after adopting a flat, attacking line.

England may have been in a desperate search for points in Rome, but Farrell kicked from hand just three times at the Stadio Olimpico. He passed 38 times and ran possession nine times, providing further evidence of his growing willingness to ask the opposing defence questions.

Points, however, still win Test matches, and Farrell's tournament haul of 64 left him just two adrift of Ireland's Jonny Sexton. Farrell added another 12 in the second Test against the All Blacks in Dunedin in the summer, taking him to 271 career Test points and to sixth on England's all-time list, after just 25 caps. Wilkinson's record haul of 1,179 may remain some way off, but the heir to the throne already has his predecessor firmly in his sights.

England
Rugby

Position: **No. 8**

Age: **22**

Height: **1.88m**

Weight: **126kg**

Caps: **12**

IN PROFILE:

Billy Vunipola

The powerful Saracens back rower made an explosive impact in what was only his first season in the senior England set-up.

England have enjoyed the services of some of the game's finest No.8s over the years, from Wavell Wakefield to Lawrence Dallaglio, and Andy Ripley to Dean Richards, but none of the legends who came before him have been quite as big, brutal and abrasive with the ball in hand as Billy Vunipola.

Size isn't everything, of course, but as a long list of bruised tacklers would testify, the Saracens forward is a beast to bring down and his destructive impact on the RBS 6 Nations before his tournament was prematurely curtailed by injury was an object lesson in how to generate forward momentum.

He marked his first England cap with a try on debut against Argentina in Salta in the summer of 2013, but it was in the 2014 RBS 6 Nations that the Red Rose were really able to harness Vunipola's power at Test level, as he rampaged his way through those brave (or foolish) enough to get in his way.

His muscular burst through the French midfield to create England's first try in Paris in February, committing three desperate defenders before timing his offload to Luther Burrell perfectly, was as unstoppable as it was direct.

The back rower was equally devastating against Scotland at Murrayfield the following week. He made a total of 58 metres in the match, 46 more than anyone else in the England pack, and it was something of a mercy to the home side when Stuart Lancaster hauled him off after 69 minutes. An ankle injury in the Ireland game ended his championship, but he was back in the thick of it in the second and third Tests in New Zealand in the summer.

The number eight will still only be 22 when the 2015 World Cup begins in England, and while there may be older and more experienced players in Stuart Lancaster's pack, few seem set to create as much blind panic in opposition ranks as the Saracens bulldozer.

IN PROFILE:

Marland Yarde

With four tries in his first five Tests, the Harlequins wing has proved himself a potent force since his debut against Argentina.

Position: **Wing**
Age: **22**
Height: **1.83m**
Weight: **95kg**
Caps: **7**

England Rugby

It is a measure of the strength of New Zealand rugby that tries against the All Blacks are something of a collector's item. The list of Englishmen who have scored against the Kiwis is not exactly lengthy, while only 11 England players to date have touched down twice in their career against the New Zealanders.

It is even rarer to score against the All Blacks in successive Tests. The first man to achieve the feat was wing Mike Harrison in 1985 in Christchurch and then in Wellington seven days later, while scrum-half Matt Dawson was a double try-scorer in the space of a week in Dunedin and Auckland 13 years later.

The most recent addition to this exclusive roll of honour is Marland Yarde, after the Harlequins wing pierced the Kiwi defence in the second Test in Dunedin and again in the third Test in Hamilton in the summer.

A debutant against Argentina in Buenos Aries in June 2013, scoring twice in the Estadio Jose Amalfitani, Yarde was denied the chance to play in the RBS 6 Nations by a persistent hip injury in early 2014, but he finally made up for lost time in New Zealand with a series of dynamic displays that underlined why he is so highly rated by the England management.

His try in Dunedin was the pick of the pair as he burst onto Danny Care's pop pass and scythed powerfully through the attempted tackles of Richie McCaw, Aaron Cruden and Jerome Kaino, while his score in Hamilton was a short-range thrust that highlighted the power the winger possesses to compliment his undoubted pace.

His overall performance in the third Test in the Waikato Stadium was his best in an England shirt to date. He led the way for England in the number of metres gained (84), defenders beaten (five) and clean breaks made (three), and whenever he had the ball in his hands, the All Blacks looked vulnerable.

Stuart Lancaster will be hoping four tries in his first seven Test appearances will merely be the *hors d'oeuvres* of Yarde's international career. The Harlequins star has proved himself against the reigning world champions in their own backyard and the suspicion is that the best is yet to come.

England Women Team of the Year

It may seem churlish to single out individuals in a year in which England lifted the World Cup. Any side that becomes world champions is one blessed with an abundance of world-class players battling for places in the starting XV.

Head Coach Gary Street certainly rang the changes during the tournament in France. All 26 of his victorious squad featured at some stage during the five games in Marcoussis and subsequently Paris, and Street did not name the same side for successive fixtures.

But, of course, there were players, both in the powerful England pack and in the back line, who delivered pivotal, eye-catching performances in France for Street and the Red Roses.

England Women celebrate victory over Ireland in the semi-finals of the 2014 World Cup in France.

IN PROFILE:

Sarah Hunter

The first name on the England team sheet, the experienced back rower was in imperious form for England throughout the year.

England Rugby

Position: **No. 8/ Flanker**
Age: **29**
Height: **1.77m**
Weight: **80kg**
Caps: **68**

The rock that underpins the England team, Sarah Hunter was in imperious form in 2014, and it spoke volumes about the Lichfield No.8's phenomenal consistency and stature within the side that she was an ever-present for the Red Rose throughout the Six Nations and World Cup campaigns.

To start all ten matches would have been a significant feat in any calendar year, but it was all the more remarkable given the circumstances, as head coach Gary Street repeatedly altered his first-choice side, resting and reassessing players and experimenting with new combinations as the World Cup final beckoned. Not once did England field the same XV, but one constant was Hunter's name on the team sheet.

She responded magnificently to the workload. Tries against Scotland in Aberdeen and Ireland at Twickenham in the championship helped England seal the Triple Crown, while she was ever-present during the World Cup in France, assuming the captaincy during the group-stage clashes against Spain and Canada and scoring the Red Rose's only try against the Canucks in the 13–13 draw in the pool.

One of 11 survivors from the heart-breaking defeat in the 2010 World Cup final, Hunter's performance in the final against the Canucks in Paris four years later was pivotal, as the England pack laid the platform up front for a cathartic 21–9 victory.

A relative late-comer to Test rugby, Hunter played rugby league at primary school before switching codes as a 14-year-old. Her journey took her to Lichfield via Loughborough Universit,y but it was not until 2007, at the age of 23, that she first pulled on the famous white shirt against Scotland in the Six Nations.

Since making her international bow, she has become the most trusted of Street's lieutenants, winning five Six Nations titles and the European Championship. Part of the side that whitewashed the Black Ferns in the three-Test series in 2012, she also captained England on their tour of New Zealand the following year.

Hunter won her 50th cap against Italy in March 2013, but despite having amassed so much experience, her central role in England's World Cup triumph was the defining moment of what is already an illustrious career.

IN PROFILE:

Kay Wilson

England's joint top try scorer at the World Cup, the Bristol flyer produced her finest season of Test rugby in 2014.

England Rugby

Position: **Wing/Full-back**
Age: **23**
Height: **1.67m**
Weight: **78kg**
Caps: **31**

Every side yearns for a try machine, a player with that innate, predatory eye for the line and, in 2014, it was flying Bristol wing Kay Wilson who stepped forward to ensure that precious five-point scores were rarely in short supply for the Red Rose.

Wilson began her Test year at full-back for the Six Nations opener against France in Grenoble, but it was when she was reinstated to the wing for the clash against Ireland at Twickenham in February that the tries began to flow, scoring in a 17–10 defeat of the Irish at HQ. A fortnight later she doubled her tally for the tournament as Wales were despatched 35–3 at the Stoop, but her championship exploits were to prove merely a warm-up for her deadly performances at the World Cup in France later in the year.

She started the tournament in fine style, registering a double in a 65–3 rout of the Samoans, and she was at her deadly best once again just four days later with a third score of the World Cup as England ran in six tries beat Spain 45–5.

The Canadian defence was able to resist Wilson's advances in the final pool game but her uncharacteristic blank owed more to the fact she was a replacement in Marcoussis, playing just 20 minutes of the contest as a second-half replacement for Katherine Merchant.

The semi-final against Ireland in the Stade Jean-Bouin, however, saw the Bristol star rediscover her priceless ability to cross the whitewash, as she improbably avoided the touchline in the tackle to dive over at the corner as England strolled to a 40–7 victory. There was no fairytale fifth try in the final in Paris against the Canadians, but her personal haul of four did make her England's joint top scorer in the tournament with Marlie Packer.

Wilson celebrated her 23rd birthday a month after the Red Rose's World Cup triumph, and with the best years of her international career ahead of her, it seems certain that the tries will continue to flow with reassuring regularity.

IN PROFILE:

Katy Mclean

The woman who lifted the World Cup for England in Paris, Mclean has been the captain of the Red Roses since 2010.

England Rugby

Position: **Fly-half**
Age: **29**
Height: **1.67m**
Weight: **70kg**
Caps: **73**

According to England head coach Gary Street, Katy Mclean is "my eyes on the pitch" and since her Test debut in 2007 the fly-half and England captain has been dutifully keeping a watching brief on proceedings for her boss.

The relationship between the coach and his playmaker has certainly proved productive. Mclean inherited the armband from Catherine Spencer in 2010, but even before she took up the leadership reins, England won three Grand Slams with the fly-half and Street in tandem. Two more Six Nations titles followed after Mclean's appointment as skipper, and the only major blemish on their joint record was the loss to New Zealand in the 2010 World Cup final. They rectified that painful setback in Paris four years later and in the same year that she was awarded an MBE for services to the game, Mclean was finally a world champion.

A product of the England Under-19, England A and England Academy set-ups, Mclean featured in four of the Red Roses' matches during the Six Nations in 2014, contributing 18 points as Street's side beat Scotland, Ireland and Wales to secure the Triple Crown.

The Darlington Mowden Park Sharks No.10 missed the final game of the championship against Italy in Rovato, when Street opted for Ceri Large at fly-half, but she returned to the starting XV for the opening game of the World Cup campaign against Samoa in Marcoussis.

Her battle with Large for the No.10 shirt continued throughout the tournament, but after her Worcester rival got the nod against Spain and Canada, Street recalled his

captain for the crucial semi-final showdown against Ireland and the all-important final against Canada.

Mclean's relationship with Street is set to change in 2015, however. The RFU's decision to make her one of 11 full-time professionals playing for England in the 2014–15 IRB Women's Sevens World Series may see her involvement in the 15-a-side game truncated, but after a year in which the duo steered England to World Cup glory, it would surely be an amicable separation.

IN PROFILE:

Marlie Packer

The dynamic Wasps flanker made a huge impact for England at the World Cup in Paris.

England Rugby

Position: **Flanker**
Age: **25**
Height: **1.65m**
Weight: **73kg**
Caps: **32**

Sport at the highest level is all about seizing opportunities when they present themselves, and Marlie Packer did just that in 2014 to ensure she was more than a bystander as England celebrated their World Cup triumph in France.

The record books will show that the Wasps flanker was England's joint top try scorer in the tournament with team-mate Kay Wilson (with four), but the story those books will not tell is just how perilously close Packer came to missing out on selection for the final.

The back-rower, voted the England Players' Player of the Year after a superb Six Nations in 2012, seemed destined to be a major player for the Red Rose at the World Cup. Three starts and a try from the bench against Ireland in the 2014 Six Nations only enhanced her reputation, and as the squad crossed the Channel in August, her place in the team looked secure.

Two tries in the 45–5 demolition of Spain in the pool stages followed, but Packer was then overlooked for the pivotal group match against Canada in favour of Heather Fisher, while Alex Matthews was selected ahead of her in the starting XV to face Ireland in the semi-final.

Packer must have feared the worst, but her tournament took a dramatic turn in the 63rd minute of the clash against Ireland, when coach Gary Street sent her into the fray in place of Maggie Alphonsi. Within seven minutes of her introduction, the Wasps forward had powered her way over for her third try of the tournament and, 60 seconds later, she made it a double after chasing a clever kick from Rachael Burford.

It was an explosive impact that Street did not ignore, and when the England XV to tackle Canada in the final was announced, Packer's name was back on the team sheet. She rewarded the coach's faith in Paris with 65 minutes of relentless work in the England back row before she was substituted, and although there was no fifth try of the tournament for the flanker, a World Cup winner's medal would have provided more than sufficient consolation.

Appearances

THE MEN WHO HAVE SET NEW MILESTONES PLAYING FOR THE RED ROSE

LEADING AMATEUR

Jason Leonard's international career spanned the amateur and professional eras, but the most-capped Englishman to have played exclusively as an amateur is Peter Winterbottom. The openside flanker made 58 Test appearances for his country between 1982 and 1993, and was in the starting XV that lost the 1991 World Cup final against Australia at Twickenham.

LONG-LASTING SHAW

The accolade of the longest England career in terms of years played belongs to second row Simon Shaw. First capped against Italy at Twickenham in November 1996, the Bristol, Wasps and Toulon lock made his 71st and final Test appearance for the Red Rose in the 2011 World Cup against France in Auckland, 15 years after he made his international bow against the *Azzurri*.

Below: **No one has made more Test appearances for England than prop Jason Leonard.**

YOUNGEST-EVER PLAYER

He may only have played a modest ten Tests, but Colin Laird still holds the distinction of being England's youngest-ever player. The Harlequins fly-half was just 18 years and 124 days old when he was capped for the first time against Wales at Twickenham in January 1927, and he was an ever-present in the side the following season when England completed the Five Nations Grand Slam.

ENGLAND'S OLDEST PLAYER

Conversely the oldest man to represent England in an international is Frederick Gilbert. The full-back was 38 years and 362 days old when he made his debut against Wales at Twickenham in 1923 and, after celebrating his 39th birthday three days later, he won his second and last cap for England the following month against Ireland in Leicester.

MOST CAPPED PLAYER

The only player to amass a century of caps for his country, Jason Leonard's 114 Test appearances is an England record that is yet to be eclipsed. The Harlequins prop was 22 when he made his international debut against Argentina in Buenos Aries in 1990, and played his last game for the Red Rose 14 years later against Italy in Rome. Leonard's record-breaking career included four World Cup campaigns, and he came off the bench in Sydney in 2003 when England beat the Wallabies to lift the Webb Ellis Cup.

CAPTAIN CARLING

England's most capped captain is Will Carling, who led the Red Rose 59 times during his career. He was first handed the armband for the clash against Australia at Twickenham in November 1988, taking over the role from scrum-half Richard Harding, and he last skippered the side against Ireland in March 1996. England won 44 of their 59 games under Carling, claiming the Five Nations Grand Slam in 1991, 1992 and 1995.

Above: **Will Carling captained the Red Rose in a record 59 internationals.**

CARLING'S RECORD-BREAKING RUN

Carling also holds the record for the most consecutive Test appearances for England, featuring in 44 successive internationals between 1989 and 1995. The centre began his remarkable run of games against Fiji at Twickenham in November 1989, and started in all of the Red Rose's next 43 games before missing out on selection for the World Cup group stage match against Italy in Durban in May 1995.

LONGEST-SERVING AMATEUR CAPTAIN

The end of Carling's reign as captain came in the professional era, and the man to lead England the most times solely in the amateur age is Bill Beaumont. The second row led the Red Rose for the first time against Wales in Cardiff in March 1977, replacing Roger Uttley as captain, and skippered the side a total of 21 times. Under his leadership, England won the championship Grand Slam in 1980.

FIRST TO 50 CAPS

The modern era has seen many players amass 50 caps for England, but the first man to reach the milestone was Rory Underwood. The prolific wing made his Test debut in a 12–9 victory over Ireland at Twickenham in February 1984 and, seven years later, he made his 50th appearance for his country as the Red Rose beat Scotland 9–6 in the World Cup semi-final at Murrayfield. Underwood went on to win a total of 85 caps for England and also represented the British & Irish Lions in six Tests.

MORE LEONARD RECORDS

Jason Leonard also holds the records for the most appearances in the championship and the World Cup. The long-serving prop played a total of 54 times in the Five and subsequently Six Nations after his championship debut against Wales in Cardiff in 1991 and he featured in 22 World Cup fixtures, beginning with the game against the All Blacks at Twickenham in 1991 and climaxing with his substitute appearance against the Wallabies in the 2003 Rugby World Cup final.

Points

THE MEN WHO HAVE SET NEW SCORING RECORDS PLAYING FOR THE RED ROSE.

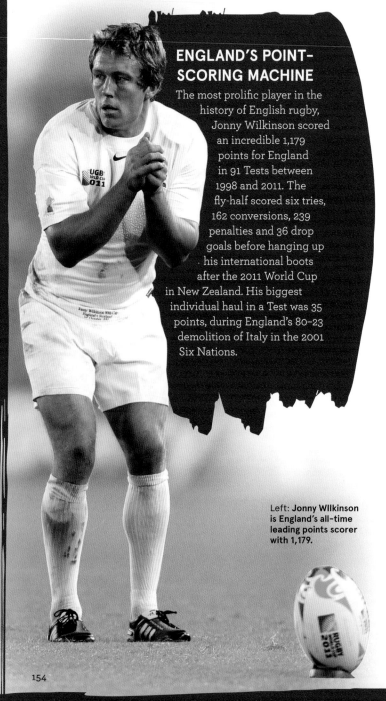

ENGLAND'S POINT-SCORING MACHINE

The most prolific player in the history of English rugby, Jonny Wilkinson scored an incredible 1,179 points for England in 91 Tests between 1998 and 2011. The fly-half scored six tries, 162 conversions, 239 penalties and 36 drop goals before hanging up his international boots after the 2011 World Cup in New Zealand. His biggest individual haul in a Test was 35 points, during England's 80–23 demolition of Italy in the 2001 Six Nations.

Left: **Jonny Wilkinson is England's all-time leading points scorer with 1,179.**

MOST POINTS IN A SINGLE MATCH

Wilkinson's haul of 35 points against the Italians was certainly impressive, but the record for the most points by an England player in a Test match is held by Sale and Saracens fly-half Charlie Hodgson. Remarkably, Hodgson set the record on his Test debut, against Romania at Twickenham in 2001, scoring two tries, 14 conversions and two penalties for a tally of 44 points.

WONDERFUL WEBB

England's most successful points-scorer of the amateur era is full-back Jonathan Webb, who notched up 296 points in 33 appearances for England. The full-back made his debut from the bench against Australia in Sydney at the inaugural World Cup in 1987, kicking a conversion, and knocked over a penalty in his last Test for England against Ireland in Dublin seven years later.

MOST TRIES IN A MATCH

Three England players jointly hold the record for the most tries in a match with five. Harlequins wing Douglas Lambert was the first Englishman to achieve the feat on his international debut against France in Richmond in 1907, while Rory Underwood emulated him in 1989 when he scored five against Fiji at Twickenham. The most recent player to cross the line five times in a match was Josh Lewsey, against Uruguay in the group stages of the 2003 World Cup in Australia.

MOST TRIES IN A SINGLE TOURNAMENT

The 1914 Championship was a good one for England as they completed the Grand Slam for the second time, and it was also a superb season for wing Cyril Lowe, who set an England record for the most tries scored in a single tournament. Lowe failed to get on the score sheet in the opening game against Wales, but he scored twice against Ireland at Twickenham before registering back-to-back hat-tricks against Scotland in Inverleith and against France in Colombes for a record haul of eight tries.

MOST TRIES AT THE WORLD CUP

Rory Underwood holds the record for the most career tries in the World Cup with 11, but Chris Ashton is the most prolific Englishman in a single tournament, scoring six times in New Zealand in 2011. The Saracens wing crossed twice in the group stage victory over Georgia in Dunedin, before recording a hat-trick in the 67–3 demolition of Romania. His final try of the tournament came in the 16–12 victory over Scotland in Auckland.

WORLD CUP HAT-TRICK HEROES

Ashton's hat-trick against the Romanians in the 2011 World Cup was the fourth by an England player at the World Cup. Wakefield wing Mike Harrison was the first man to register a treble, crossing three times in the 60–7 victory over Japan in Sydney in the 1987 tournament. Josh Lewsey scored five against Uruguay in Brisbane in 2003, while Mark Cueto scored three against Romania in Dunedin eight years later.

WORLD CUP LEADING POINTS-SCORER

Unsurprisingly, Jonny Wilkinson is England's all-time highest points-scorer in both 6 Nations championship and World Cup matches. The fly-half accumulated 546 points in 5 and 6 Nations games, while he scored 277 points at four separate World Cups. Wilkinson scored 69 points in the 1999 tournament, while he was at his most prolific in Australia in 2003, with 113 points. The 2007 World Cup saw him score 67 points, while his swansong tournament – in New Zealand in 2011 – yielded 28 points in four games.

MOST POINTS IN A WORLD CUP MATCH

Wilkinson holds a plethora of England scoring records, but the man to have landed the most conversions in a Test match is Northampton fly-half Paul Grayson. The Saints star was part of the side that routed the Netherlands 110–0 in a one-sided World Cup qualifier in Huddersfield in November 1998, converting a staggering 15 of England's 16 tries.

Above: **Rory Underwood scored a record-breaking 49 tries in just 85 Tests for England.**

England Team Records

THE COLLECTIVE MILESTONES SET BY THE RED ROSE

AMATEUR SUCCESS

England's most successful sequence in the amateur era came in the 19th century, when the team won ten games on the bounce. The record-breaking run began with a victory over Wales in Swansea in December 1882 and, after nine more triumphs, it was ended when they were held to a draw by Scotland in Edinburgh in March 1886.

RECORD-BREAKING 6 NATIONS

Although England narrowly missed out on the Grand Slam, the 2001 RBS 6 Nations championship was the most prolific in the team's history as the side accumulated 229 points en route to the title. The Red Rose despatched Wales (44–15), Italy (80–23), Scotland (43–3) and France (48–19) before Ireland eventually beat them 20–14 in Dublin.

Below: England's 15–13 victory against the All Blacks in Wellington in 2003 was part of a record-breaking winning run.

NO PLACE LIKE HOME

Twickenham is frequently referred to as a fortress, and between 1999 and 2004 it certainly lived up to its reputation, as England went 22 games unbeaten at home. The phenomenal run began with a 101–10 rout of Tonga in the group stages of the World Cup and included a hat-trick of wins over both the Wallabies and the Springboks as well as a 31–28 victory over the All Blacks. The record-breaking sequence included 113 tries and a total of 1,024 points and was finally brought to an end in March 2004 following a 19–13 loss to Ireland – also notable for being England's first defeat as the reigning world champions.

RECORD-BREAKING RUN

England's longest winning sequence in the professional era is 14 games, a run that began with a 50–10 demolition of Wales at Twickenham in March 2002. The streak included wins over the All Blacks, Wallabies and Springboks on consecutive weekends at Twickenham in November later that year and a famous 15–13 victory over New Zealand in Wellington in June 2003, before it was finally brought to an end when the Red Rose were beaten 17–16 by France in August in a World Cup warm-up match in Marseille. The run saw England amass 493 points, scoring 40 or more points in half of the matches.

TRY FRENZY

England also scored a record 29 tries in the 2001 campaign. They scored six against Wales in Cardiff, ten against Italy at Twickenham and six more against Scotland in London. Another six came against the French at HQ and there was one more in the defeat to Ireland in Dublin. Will Greenwood led the way with six tries, including a hat-trick in the Millennium Stadium, while Iain Balshaw went over five times during the season.

SUCCESS IN THE EMERALD ISLE

Ireland is also England's favourite country away from home, with the Red Rose running out winners in 32 of their 65 visits to the Emerald Isle.

BIGGEST WIN

The biggest win in England's Test history was their 134–0 destruction of Romania at Twickenham in November 2001. The one-sided rout at Twickenham featured 20 tries, with Jason Robinson scoring four and Ben Cohen and Dan Luger both registering hat-tricks, while Charlie Hodgson landed 14 conversions and two penalties.

MOST CONSECUTIVE 6 NATIONS WINS

The Red Rose record for the most consecutive wins in the 4/5/6 Nations is ten and was set in the 1920s. The sequence began in the final match of the 1922 4 Nations, when England beat Scotland 11–5 at Twickenham. Back-to-back Grand Slams in 1923 and 1924 extended the winning run to nine, and it reached double figures when Wavell Wakefield's team despatched Wales 12–6 at HQ in the opening game of the 1925 championship. It finally came to an end when England were held to a 6–6 draw by Ireland at Twickenham the following month.

ENGLAND SHOW THEIR MEAN STREAK

The 2003 6 Nations saw Clive Woodward's side clinch the Grand Slam and it was also the campaign in which England conceded the fewest points in a 6 Nations season. The Red Rose leaked just four tries in five games and 46 points in total. France were the only side to record double figures against England in the competition, going down 25–17 at Twickenham in February.

Above: Charlie Hodgson scored 44 points in England's 134–0 rout of Romania in 2001.

FAMILIAR FOE

England's first-ever international opponents were Scotland, the two sides crossing swords for the first time in 1871 in Edinburgh, but England have recorded their most Test victories against Ireland. The first Anglo-Irish game was staged at the Oval in 1875 and in the 128 games the two nations have played in all competitions up to the end of the 2014 RBS 6 Nations, England had won 74 times.

JOY ON TOUR

England's longest winning run in tour matches is seven. It began in June 2000 when the Red Rose beat South Africa 27–22 in Bloemfontein. A two-Test triumph over Canada and a win over the USA Eagles in San Francisco in 2001 followed, and there was then a 26–18 success against Argentina in Buenos Aries in June 2002. In 2003, the Red Rose came home from Wellington and Melbourne with victories over the All Blacks and Wallabies respectively, and the sequence was only broken when New Zealand beat Clive Woodward's side in Dunedin in June 2004.

SLAYING THE SPRINGBOKS

The southern hemisphere heavyweights of South Africa, New Zealand and Australia invariably provide stern opposition, and England's biggest victory over any of three came against the Springboks at Twickenham in November 2002. The Red Rose ran in seven unanswered tries, two from centre Will Greenwood, in a 53-3 romp. Their biggest victory over Australia came in 2010 when the Wallabies were beaten 35-18, while their highest score against New Zealand was the 38-21 triumph at HQ in 2012.

LEVEL PEGGING

In the 676 Test matches England had played up to the end of the 2014 RBS 6 Nations, the Red Rose had been involved in 50 draws. Their highest scoring draw was the 26-26 stalemate with the All Blacks at Twickenham in December 1997.

MOST DRAWS

Of those 50 draws in Tests, the most have come against Scotland, with a record 18 stalemates in the 132 Tests played between the two countries. The first Anglo-Scottish match to finish level was the pointless meeting in Glasgow in 1873, while the most recent was the 15-15 result in the RBS 6 Nations at Murrayfield in 2010.

TRIPLE CROWNS AND GRAND SLAMS

England hold the record for both the most Grand Slams and Triple Crowns in the history of the championship. The side's clean sweep in the 2003 RBS 6 Nations was England's 12th Grand Slam, while victories over Scotland, Ireland and Wales in 2014 gave the Red Rose a record 24th Triple Crown.

SOUTHERN HEMISPHERE SCALPS

Few sides return from the southern hemisphere victorious and England are the only one of the Home Union countries to have registered victories against South Africa, New Zealand and Australia away from home. The Red Rose beat the Springboks 18-9 in Johannesburg in June 1972 and the following year they travelled to Auckland and beat the All Blacks 16-10. England had to wait until 2003 until they recorded their first victory over the Wallabies on Australian soil, finally emerging 25-14 victors from the game in Melbourne.

BREAKING THE CENTURY MARK

England have surpassed the 100-point mark five times in Test matches. The 110-0 rout of the Netherlands in 1998 was their first international century, and they achieved it twice against the USA and Tonga the following year. Romania were despatched 134-0 in 2001, while England's most recent three-figure score came in 2003, when Uruguay were demolished 111-13 at the 2003 World Cup in Australia.

Above: England's 53-3 triumph against South Africa in 2002 was their biggest-ever victory against the Springboks.

BEST WORLD CUP WINNING STREAK

England's longest winning run in World Cup matches stands at eight. Seven of the victories came in the 2003 tournament in Australia as the Red Rose lifted the Webb Ellis Cup, and when the defending champions beat the USA Eagles in Lens in the opening game of the 2007 competition, it was extended to eight.

ITALY ARE TO ENGLAND'S LIKING

In terms of winning percentage, Italy are England's opposition of choice, with the Red Rose recording victories in all 20 meetings between the two teams. The Red Rose first played the *Azzurri* at Twickenham in the 1991 World Cup, winning 36–6 courtesy of a brace of tries from Jeremy Guscott, while their most recent triumph was their 52–11 success in Rome in the 2014 RBS 6 Nations.

Below: **Josh Lewsey touches down for one of his five tries against Uruguay at the 2003 World Cup.**

6 NATIONS SUCCESS

England are the most successful side in the history of the 6 Nations. By the end of the 2014 tournament, the Red Rose had won 51 of 75 matches played, placing them one clear of France. They are also the most prolific side in terms of both tries (214) and points (2,061) scored.

BIGGEST AWAY WIN

While the 111–13 romp against Uruguay at the 2003 World Cup was the Red Rose's biggest-ever victory outside England, Brisbane was deemed a neutral venue. The side's biggest win in an "away" fixture came against Italy in the inaugural 6 Nations in 2000. England scored eight tries in the Stadio Flaminio in Rome, including a hat-trick from Austin Healy, as they ran out 59–12 winners.

ENGLAND TOO STRONG FOR URUGUAY

England's triumphant 2003 World Cup campaign featured the side's biggest-ever victory in the tournament – a 111–13 rout of Uruguay in Brisbane in Pool C. The Red Rose scored 17 tries in the victory over the South Americans, with Josh Lewsey scoring five and Iain Balshaw, Mike Catt, Andy Gomarsall and Jason Robinson all crossing twice.

Credits

The publishers would like to thank the following sources for their kind permission to reproduce the pictures in this book.

ACTION IMAGES: /Graham Stuart: 124

CORBIS: /G Piazzolla/Demotix: 87

GETTY IMAGES: 104-105; /Anthony Au-Yeung: 52; /Steve Bardens/The RFU Collection: 11, 60R; /Shaun Botterill: 17L, 24, 28, 29R, 34, 57, 129, 131, 158; /Simon Bruty: 132, 133R; /David Cannon: 25R, 27, 30L, 85, 157; /Russell Cheyne: 153, 155; /Harry Engels: 76; /Julian Finney: 110-111, 116, 117; /Stu Forster: 25L, 29L, 120-121,122; /Laurence Griffiths: 20R, 60L, 69; /Richard Heathcote: 64L; /Mike Hewitt: 8-9, 62, 63, 82-83, 84, 86, 90; /Martin Hunter: 47L, 49; /Mark Kolbe: 126-127; /Jan Kruger/The RFU Collection: 149; /Matthew Lewis: 40, 128; /Jordan Mansfield: 72-73, 74-75, 77, 78, 79, 81, 89, 91L, 91R, 146-147, 148, 150, 151; /Tony Marshall: 101; /Tony Marshall/The RFU Collection: 108, 119; /Ethan Miller: 106; /Francois Nel: 115; /Jason Oxenham: 97; /Hannah Peters: 10, 43L, 92-93, 94-95, 96, 98, 114; /Adam Pretty: 135, 159; /David Rogers: 7, 12-13, 16, 17R, 18, 19, 20L, 21, 22, 23, 37, 38-39, 42, 43R, 45, 46, 47R, 48, 50L 50R, 53, 54, 55, 70, 133L, 136-137, 152, 154, 156; /David Rogers/The RFU Collection: 4-5, 14-15, 26, 30R, 32, 33L, 33R, 35, 58-59, 64R, 66, 67, 71T, 71C, 71B, 130, 138-139, 140, 141, 142, 143, 144, 145, 160; /Cameron Spencer: 102-103, 107; /Simon Watts: 44

PRESS ASSOCIATION IMAGES: /Joe Giddens: 112-113

REX FEATURES: /David Gibson/Fotosport: 125

Every effort has been made to acknowledge correctly and contact the source and/or copyright holder of each picture and Carlton Books Limited apologises for any unintentional errors or omissions, which will be, corrected in future editions of this book.